Preaching to Strangers

Preaching to Strangers

William H. Willimon
and Stanley Hauerwas

Westminster/John Knox Press
Louisville, Kentucky

Except where otherwise marked, scripture quotations are from the Revised Standard Version of the Bible, copyright 1946, 1952, © 1971, 1973 by the Division of Christian Education of the National Council of the Churches of Christ in the U.S.A. and are used by permission.

Scripture quotations marked NRSV are from the New Revised Standard Version of the Bible, copyright © 1989 by the Division of Christian Education of the National Council of the Churches of Christ in the U.S.A., and are used by permission.

Book design by Kristin Dietrich

First edition

This book is printed on acid-free paper that meets the American National Standards Institute Z39.48 standard. ∞

Published by Westminster/John Knox Press
Louisville, Kentucky

PRINTED IN THE UNITED STATES OF AMERICA
9 8 7 6 5 4 3 2 1

Library of Congress Cataloging-in-Publication Data

Willimon, William H.
  Preaching to strangers : evangelism in today's world / William H. Willimon and Stanley Hauerwas. — 1st ed.
        p.   cm.
  Includes bibliographical references.
  ISBN 0-664-25105-6 (pbk. : alk. paper)

  1. Methodist Church—Sermons.   2. Sermons, American.
3. Preaching.   4. Willimon, William H.   I. Hauerwas, Stanley,
1940–   . II. Title.
BX8333.W46P74   1992
252′.076—dc20   92-3950

Contents

Preface

Our lives are made up of accidents. It was by sheer happenstance that we both arrived at Duke at the same time. It was by happenstance that we both came under the influence of Karl Barth at Yale Divinity School. It was by happenstance that we discovered we really liked to work together and that two strangers became good friends. But all these "accidents" are the stuff of our lives.

That our lives are so constituted, of course, has much to do with the character of this book. For it is our belief that through the church our lives are given greater coherence than we could ever supply from within our own experiences. It is through the preaching ministry of the church that we find our lives so narrated. If we are lucky, our lives are made more than they would be by others who claim us. In some fundamental ways, what it means to be the church is to have our lives made vulnerable to those who would make us God's.

We owe many our heartfelt thanks for making it possible for us to write this book together. Mrs. Gay Trotter and Mrs. Jacqueline Andrews have, as usual, managed to take Willimon's text and Hauerwas's text and somehow bring them together. These are the real heroines of this tale. Our many colleagues and students are a constant source of support and influence whom we could not live without. We dedicate this book in particular to Brenda Brodie, faithful listener at Duke Chapel.

Introduction

This book began with an invitation for Willimon to put together a collection of his sermons. Knowing that the world does not need another collection of sermons, or his sermons, at least, Willimon thought it might be interesting for us to write the book together. Oftentimes after hearing Willimon preach, I made it my job to give him holy hell about what he should have said instead of what he did say. So he suggested that we formalize the procedure and that I respond to a series of his sermons.

We originally thought we might organize the book around the church year. So Will went through his sermons written since coming to Duke that correlated to the Christian year. I read through them but found I could not respond. Of course, part of the problem was that I was busy with other projects and there was always "something else to do." But something was missing. I suspect what was missing is the same thing missing in any collection of sermons, and the reason that we do not need another. The written sermon is a different genre from the sermon preached. There is much to be said for the written sermon, but we must realize that when the sermon appears in a book, something seems missing. It is like the recognition that when Paul wrote his letters they were letters, but as they appear in the New Testament they are no longer letters, but scripture. In that case the letters have become more than they were, but in the case of the sermon it often becomes less.

I was able to get under way on this book by happenstance. Too lazy to go to church one Sunday, I listened to Will on the radio. I suddenly discovered that I had something to tell him that had to do with the delivery of the sermon. It was the live word, even through the radio, that stirred me to action. So, rather than being a book shaped by the Christian year, which would have been preferable in many ways, this book is my response to a series of Will's sermons through the first part of the school year in 1991. There are at once strengths and weaknesses to this approach, some of which I will outline below, but at least the reader has a feeling for the inextricably dramatic character of the sermon—dramatic in the sense that a sermon must elicit a response from hearers, or in this case a hearer, to be a sermon. We hope that this book, to some extent at least, carries something of that drama.

I must admit that as we began the process I was a bit worried that Will might start preparing his sermons with my response in mind. Any experienced teacher knows that no matter how experienced we are, when one of our colleagues appears in the classroom it is very hard to resist lecturing to that person rather than to the students. I was afraid that Will might start responding to my criticisms, which I gave him week after week, and begin to try to counter them in the next sermon. I should have known better, however, as he is far too experienced and strong-willed to worry about a theologian. Again I shall try to say below why that is a very good thing for understanding the relationship between preaching and theology.

My difficulty in responding to the sermon as text is but a reminder of how important context is for the church's preaching ministry. Therefore, it is important that I try to make clear Willimon's context. He is Dean of the Chapel at Duke University. For those unfamiliar with Duke, the Chapel is a commanding Gothic building in the center of the West Campus. Mr. Duke thought that a university ought to look like Princeton, so Duke is neo-neo-neo-Gothic. It is a new university's attempt to become instantly traditional. The Chapel itself is a magnificent Gothic structure which, since we were Methodists, must be called a chapel. After all, Methodists do not have cathedrals.

Though the Chapel is the central symbol of Duke used on almost all our official publications, the relationship between Duke as a university and the Chapel is ambiguous at best. Administrators at Duke often say that the Chapel is a symbol of the "spiritual" dimension of all knowledge, which certainly seems to be a long way from the presumption that the Chapel is where we worship the Trinity. I do not mean to suggest that there is bad will about the Chapel among administrators, faculty, and/or students at Duke. Rather it is just that no one is sure what to do with it. It is like an archaeological shard left over from the past that is a delightful relic we would not want to eliminate, but which we do not know what to do with. In effect, the Chapel is a living fossil.

Of course, religion is almost impossible to kill in the South, and so attendance at the Chapel is remarkably good. On almost any Sunday you can count on the Chapel being filled. During Holy Week you have to get there extremely early to get a seat. This is due partly to the Chapel's tremendous music program. The Chapel choir is rightly renowned for its musical ability. Moreover, the Chapel oftentimes uses brass instruments to complement the superb organ, and the result is a kind of pageantry unknown among most Protestants.

The Chapel as a building is magnificent.[1] The stained glass is extraordinary for a modern building. In effect, the

3

building as well as the music dwarfs the preaching ministry. The word is not only hard to hear, it is lost amid the many sensory impressions.

But Willimon, who is physically short anyway, does a wonderful job of not letting the preaching ministry be entirely subordinated to the building and music. He is an excellent preacher, combining the Southerner's gift of storytelling with a sense of the integrity of theological discourse. He is not afraid to be entertaining, as he knows a sermon by being dull is not thereby automatically profound. Moreover, he has a wonderful sense of the limits and possibilities of preaching at Duke Chapel.

For example, in conversation he once suggested to me that he looked upon the Chapel as an extraordinary evangelistic tent. Every Sunday he has the opportunity to preach salvation and hope that some are converted. It is a wonderful image that suggests that Willimon knows that if the preaching ministry of the church is to be sustained at Duke it can be so only to the extent that it knows it is free. By free I mean that the ministry cannot be determined by the presuppositions that sustain Duke University.

The image of evangelistic tent with its extraordinary Gothic structure also rightly suggests the character of the congregation. Indeed the very word "congregation" is probably too strong, as Willimon strictly has no congregation, though there is a lively congregation formed as part of Duke Chapel; but, rather, his ministry is fundamentally preaching to strangers. If the Chapel is usually full, it is so because it is filled by strangers. There is a core group of people who are always there. But the congregation is largely made up of students and tourists, a metaphor we believe describes most Christians today.

The tourists come in all shapes and sizes. Some are quite literally tourists, who have come to see the building and what a service of worship in the building is like. They are there one time and never return. They may or may not be Christians. Others are "tourists" in relationship to Christianity. They come to the Chapel exactly because they can be there while preserving their anonymity. They can come, hear the beautiful music, hear an intelligent sermon, and leave without really having to deal with other people and/or their own relationship to the Christian faith. These tourists may come often.

The image of tourist or stranger to characterize the congregation is perhaps most determinatively embodied by Willimon's "audience," made up of so many students. The students are quite literally passing through. The Chapel can mean many things to them. It may mean that they confront a form of Christianity that they had no idea existed, given their "home" church. It may mean that they, by coming to chapel, are trying desperately to maintain some continuity with their religious background. Or it just may mean that they like music.

Such characterizations could go on indefinitely, but I think the most determinative explanation of what it means for Willimon to have to preach to strangers is that he is preaching to people who share no common tradition. The Greeks assumed that a stranger had a very distinct moral status. What it meant to be Greek was that you shared the same stories and around civic occasions you could tell those stories with understanding and appreciation. Strangers were those people who did not necessarily share your stories, but who seemed capable of hearing your stories and appreciating them with understanding. The stranger could be invited to join the Greek's civic festivals and might even contribute to Greek life by introducing new stories that could be made part of the Greek tradition. Barbarians, for the Greeks, were simply those who were incapable of hearing the stories of the Greeks, and thus one's only obligation to them was to kill them. Christians,

5

of course, are people who live in a world where, in their view, there are many strangers but no barbarians. Willimon's preaching is the attempt to share the gospel with strangers.

There is no question that there are special challenges to his situation. Certainly being in an academic context makes a difference in how he must address these particular strangers. The fact that he is not, Sunday after Sunday, preaching to the same people whom he has come to know and love certainly makes a difference. Normally the preaching ministry of the church takes place not in a tent where there is an audience, but rather in a place constituted by a congregation. A congregation cannot be strangers to one another, not because they know one another well, but because they have all had the same baptism. Such a people at least share enough to be capable of mounting a good argument. For better or worse, however, Willimon must preach to people who have so little in common they are not even able to locate disagreements, much less have an argument.

Yet I think it is the case, and part of the justification of this book, that *most preaching in the Christian church today is done before strangers.* For the church finds itself in a time when people have accepted the odd idea that Christianity is largely what they do with their own subjectivities. Politically we live in social orders that assume the primary task is how to achieve cooperation between strangers.[2] Indeed we believe our freedom depends on remaining fundamentally strangers to one another. We bring those habits to church, and as a result we do not share fundamentally the story of being God's creatures, but rather, if we share any story at all, it is that we are our own creators.[3] Christians once understood that they were pilgrims. Now, we are just tourists who happen to find ourselves on the same bus.

So in watching Willimon preach to strangers we may learn something in general about how preaching is to be done in the church today. I think it is very dangerous to preach to strangers, as my responses following Willimon's sermons will, I hope, exhibit. For the minister is constantly tempted to reductionist strategy for making the Christian gospel intelligible, rather than helping strangers to discover through the gospel why their lives are unintelligible.

For example, the premiere text for modern preaching is Paul Tillich's Preface to *The Shaking of the Foundations.* There Tillich said:

There are two reasons why I agree to the publication of a book of sermons at this time. Many of my students and friends outside the seminary have told me of the difficulty they have met in trying to penetrate my theological thought. They believe that through my sermons the practical or, more exactly, the existential implications of my theology are more clearly manifest. I should like to think that the sermons included here help to show that the strictly systematic character of a theology does not need to prevent it from being "practical"—that is to say: applicable to the personal and social problems of our religious life.

There is however, a more important reason for the publication of this volume. A large part of the congregation at the Sunday services came from outside the Christian circle in the most radical sense of the phrase. For them, a sermon in traditional Biblical terms would have no meaning. Therefore, I was obliged to seek a language which expresses in other terms the human experience to which the Biblical and ecclesial terminology point. In this situation, an "apologetic" type sermon has been developed. And, since I believe that this is generally the situation in which the Christian message has to be pronounced today, I hope that the publication of some attempt to meet this situation may not be useless.[4]

Notice it is Tillich's presumption that he must constantly find a way to "translate" the language of the gospel, to map the language of the gospel, onto experiences that are already well understood.[5] One must say, moreover, he did it brilliantly. He was particularly effective for audiences not unlike that of Willimon, as he made it possible for them to assume their concern for their own significance, their "ultimate concern," was in fact at the heart of what Christian faith was about. Thus the inherent narcissism of the high-culture bourgeoisie was not fundamentally challenged by the gospel of Christ.

In *The Nature of Doctrine,* George Lindbeck has characterized positions like that of Tillich as experimental-expressivist views of religion. He draws on Lonergan's account of religion to characterize experimental-expressivism. It is constituted by the following presuppositions:

1. Different religions are diverse expressions or objectifications of a common co-experience. It is this experience which identifies them as religious.

2. Experience, while conscious, may be unknown on the level of self-conscious reflection.

3. It is present in all human beings.

4. In most religions, the experience is a source and norm of objectifications: it is by reference to the experience that the adequacy or lack of adequacy is to be judged.

A fifth point characterizes a primordial religious experience as "God's gift of love" or, when fully present, as a "dynamic state of being" and "love without restrictions" and "without an object."[6]

At the heart of the experimental-expressivist project is a fear of otherness. Recognizing that we are all strangers, we then look for what we might all share in common. Of course this is also crucial for the apologetic strategy exemplified by Tillich, a strategy that seems so unavoidable given the current condition of Christianity. If the preacher cannot assume that we share practices commensurate with the gospel, then what will provide the context that makes preaching possible in the first place? We must remember that as important as what and how the preacher says what he or she has to say are the habits that constitute the "ears" that will hear what is said. In a decisive sense, preaching can be only as good as those ears make possible.

That so many preachers are possessed by Tillich-like presupposition about preaching is certainly understandable given the fact that Christianity must exist in a buyer's market. People come to church to have confirmed what they think they already know. It is almost impossible, therefore, to resist making the sermon serve to confirm our experience rather than to challenge the presumption that we even understand what it is we assumed we have experienced. Ironically, this is as true of so-called conservatives as it is of so-called liberals within the contemporary theological alternatives. Both liberals' and conservatives' strategies work to confirm different social classes' accounts of their experience.

As a result, it is almost impossible for the preacher to challenge the subtle accommodationist mode of most Christian preaching. We accommodate the hearers by trying to make the sermon fit their established habits of understanding, which only underwrites the further political accommodation of the church to the status quo. Any suggestion that in order to even begin understanding the sermon would require a transformation of our lives, particularly our economic and political habits, is simply considered unthinkable.

In such a context, preaching becomes not proclamation of news that is otherwise unavailable, but rather a form of apologetics that is meant to confirm what the hearer already knows.[7] In contrast to the apologetic mode, Lindbeck provides what he calls a cultural linguistic account of religion. By that he means:

Religions are seen as comprehensive interpretive schemes, usually embodied in myths or narratives and heavily ritualized, which structure human experience and understanding of self and world.[8]

The cultural linguistic mode assumes that apologetics can never be the first movement within Christian preaching. Rather, preaching must be understood as a practice that requires transformation on the part of preacher and hearer alike. So understood, preaching is not a matter of apologetics but rather of evangelization. That is, preaching must be understood as part of the whole church's ministry to convert our lives by having them constituted by a narrative that we have not chosen, but which has chosen us.

I think there are serious difficulties with Lindbeck's typology; indeed I think there are serious difficulties with the very notion of typology.[9] Yet his categories heuristically help us understand the tension in Willimon's sermons. Willimon is trying very hard to be an evangelist, but he keeps slipping into the apologetic mode. He does so because he so desperately wants to communicate the gospel, but the very notion of "communication" can be extremely misleading for helping us understand how we must preach today. For the notion of communication too often assumes that what one person has to say to another must "in principle" be capable of being understood. The hearer may have to work at it. Certain words may need explaining, and so on, but finally the speaker will be able to make himself or herself understood. In that sense preaching is not about communicating, but is rather to challenge our presumption of our "understanding." That is particularly the case when one is preaching to strangers. Preaching is meant to challenge the presumption that our "understanding" is sufficient to hear the gospel. Preaching rightly requires us to be transformed if we are to hear what is being proclaimed.

It will be obvious from my responses to Willimon's sermons that I admire what he is about. Willimon constantly struggles to help people feel the oddness of Christian discourse. He is about helping us see how the language Christians use only makes sense within the context of certain fundamental practices that constitute the church. He attempts to put the hearer in the contexts that make it possible for scripture to narrate our lives. He does that through engaging in quite sophisticated forms of redescription.[10] He understands that the gospel does not provide a better explanation about human existence, but rather a different description, which we are invited to learn.

Yet in the process of redescription, he is tempted to slip into the Tillichian mode of explanation. We will see that in particular when, as he often does, he tends to "existentialize" the parables so that they lose their eschatological context. It is hard to insist on the eschatological structure of our faith when you are preaching to people who do not know that they are a pilgrim church; that is, that they exist in a different time from those who have not received Christ's baptism. That is why I often remind him that his preaching is limited by his context, since worship in Duke Chapel is not always climaxed by the Eucharist.

That brings us back, of course, to some of the issues I raised at the beginning of this Introduction. To concentrate on the sermon abstracted from its locus in the total setting of worship, to concentrate on a short series of sermons separated from their context in the whole Christian year, and to abstract the sermons from a church's whole ministry is fundamentally to distort them. The very insufficiency of the sermon on certain Sundays may, as a matter of fact, make the hymn we sing all that much more powerful. So the very form of this book is a kind of distortion, but we hope it will still be of some aid to all of us who must preach and hear as strangers.

In particular we hope that the book may suggest an old and very new way to think about theological work within the church. Too often modern theology is assumed to be the reflection of creative minds that attempt to make theological discourse meaningful after it has fundamentally lost its meaning. As one who thinks that the least interesting thing about discourse is its meaning, I want decisively to challenge that notion of theology. Theology cannot make discourse work that is not working by providing it with a better metaphysics and/or theory of existence. When Tillich suggests that the "strictly systematic" character of theology does not prevent application to personal and social problems, you have a good indication that something has gone decisively wrong. For such a theology is but an abstraction, or negatively an ideology, because it is separated from the material conditions we call "church." Theology's task is not to be more truthful than preaching; rather, the function of theology is to provide a series of reminders about how the discourse is meant to work if it is to be in good working order. Theologians cannot and should not tell preachers what to preach, as theology is a servant to the preaching ministry of the church. Prayer is the most truthful form Christian conviction can take.

That does not mean that I cannot, as a theologian, have views, as will be obvious from my responses to Willimon's sermons, about the theological presumptions embodied in a sermon or a series of sermons. But it does mean that I must be mindful of the fact that Willimon's sermons are not his sermons, but are the sermons of the church. Preaching as a practice of the church makes theology possible, not vice versa.

That said, however, I think that one of the criticisms that can be made of this book is that it is perhaps too controlled by Willimon's sermons. For example, I wish Willimon would more often preach on more straightforwardly "doctrinal" issues. For example, he recently preached on the preexistence of Christ. I must admit I think we need more of that kind of preaching, as its virtue is that it lacks almost all existential relevance to people's immediate lives. But in the process we are reminded as faithful followers of Christ that our salvation is cosmic in scope, and that is just the wonder of it.

I also wish his sermons dealt more directly with the "politics" of modernity. I think as part of his redescriptions he needs to help us find the imaginative skills to resist the narratives that so grip our lives—for example, that the United States in 1991 was responding to aggression against Kuwait. Politically he might well enter into the debates concerning the nature and activities of the contemporary university, such as the presumption that the university is fundamentally apolitical. Christians have a stake in challenging such illusions to the extent that they tempt us to serve false gods.[11]

That this book has been possible, of course, results from no strong theories about theology and/or preaching. Rather the book is possible because Willimon and I are friends. There are few people I enjoy more than Willimon, as I know of no others who are able more completely to disguise their complexity. Though we enjoy each other, however, friendship cannot be sustained as an end in itself. Rather, friendship grows from attempts at common activity which we believe to be significant. In that sense too I hope that this book exemplifies the kind of friendship the church makes possible, as Will and I must learn to expose our limits to the greater glories of God's church. Certainly Will has taken the greater risk in the doing of this book and for that we are all in his debt.

STANLEY M. HAUERWAS

NOTES

1. In testimony to the building's beauty, several quite impressive books have been produced showing the Chapel in its most photogenic light. See, for example, *The Chapel, Duke University* (Durham, N.C.: Gothic Bookshop, 1986).

2. See, for example, Michael Ignatieff, *The Needs of Strangers* (New York: Viking Press, 1984).

3. This assertion obviously involves sound issues in social and political theory that has shaped modernity. My way of putting the matter is that the story of modernity is that we should have no story except the story that we've chosen when we had no story. We call the latter position freedom. The only difficulty is, we fail to note that the story that we should have no story except the story we've chosen from the position of freedom is not a story that we have chosen. In effect, modernity is the project that attempts to make our so-called freedom our fate. We cannot avoid being choosers of our own selves, but as a result we fail to note how we have been chosen by others. For a further development of this, see my book *After Christendom* (Nashville: Abingdon Press, 1991).

4. Paul Tillich, *The Shaking of the Foundations* (New York: Charles Scribner's Sons, 1948), Preface. I am in the Rev. Charles Campbell's debt for calling my attention to Tillich's Preface as well as other extraordinarily valuable suggestions for how this introduction might be done.

5. The very notion of translation is an extremely complex one. See, for example, Alasdair MacIntyre's account of the issues in his *Whose Justice? Which Rationality?* (Notre Dame, Ind.: University of Notre Dame Press, 1988), pp. 370–388.

6. George Lindbeck, *The Nature of Doctrine: Religion and Theology in a Postliberal Age* (Philadelphia: Westminster Press, 1984), p. 31.

7. "Confirm what the hearer already knows" is probably a too weak way to put the issue. For it is not just what we know, but the practices that shape what we know, that we wish to have confirmed. For example, most Americans do not wish to have called into question their loyalty to the United States of America as a necessary condition for their hearing the gospel. As a result, we lose exactly the kind of critical edge so necessary for the gospel to be preached and heard.

8. Lindbeck, p. 32.

9. Too often typologies turn out to be disguised arguments. Lindbeck on the whole, I think, avoids that temptation, though obviously his types to some extent distort positions so typed. My deeper worry about Lindbeck's strategy, however, is his assumption that the category "religion" is intelligible.

10. The notion of redescription I borrow, of course, from the work of Hans Frei. See in particular Frei's "An Afterword: Eberhard Busch's Biography of Karl Barth," in *Karl Barth in Review,* edited by Martin Romscheidt (Pittsburgh: Pickwick Press, 1981). The interrelationship between the eschatological perspective and the necessity of redescription are as complex as they are important. If Christians believe through baptism we have been made part of a new order and a new time, it means that how we understand the history in which we find ourselves embodied will, of necessity, be quite different from the understanding of those who do not believe our existence is destined by God.

11. Among the articles about Willimon and his preaching see, "Does Willimon Make Sense?" William Sachs, *The Christian Century,* April 19, 1989, pp. 412–414; "The Prince and the Preacher," Martin Copenhaver, *The Christian Ministry,* July–August, 1990, pp. 12–16; and "Pumping Truth to a Disinclined World," Marshall Shelly and Jim Berkley, *Leadership,* Spring 1990, pp. 128–137.

Freedom

Seventh Sunday in Easter
Acts 16:16–40

*"The foundations of the prison were shaken;
and immediately all the doors were opened
and every one's fetters were unfastened."*

"One thing that I like about living in New York," he said, "as opposed to where you live, is the freedom. Here there is freedom to live the life-style I choose—to eat where I want and to dress as I like. Freedom."

Then he closed his door behind us. He locked the latch, turned the dead bolt, inserted the chain, and switched on the electronic alarm, telling me, "Don't dare open that door without switching off the alarm or all hell will break loose and the cops may shoot you dead."

If there is one virtue on which we can all join hands this morning it is freedom. We Americans may disagree on taxes, national defense, policy in Central America, and whether the crust is better at Pizza Hut or Pizza Inn, but we all agree that freedom is good. Freedom of religion. Freedom of choice.

17

I have something called a "freedom phone." Most calls on this telephone sound as if they are being made in Moscow, but I don't mind. How wonderful to be free to receive calls while standing in the street in front of my house!

"And the truth shall make you free," was carved in big letters over the entrance to our high school. *Veritas vos liberabit.* I thought it was something that the principal thought up—a sign like No Smoking in the Boys' Rest Room. But no, it's in the Bible.

And while we sometimes played loose with the truth at my high school, my, how we clung to our freedom. Freedom—that blessed quest of adolescence! Freedom to have the car to go where I want and to do what I want. Freedom not to account for comings and goings to Mama and Daddy.

Freedom—the blessed treasure of academia. Here at Duke, "The Basset Affair" was a landmark case for academic freedom in this country—freedom to think, teach, and publish.

Freedom of the pulpit—freedom to speak as I feel led by God to speak.

Academic freedom? Free to rehash my yellowed old notes rather than to prepare for class. Freedom from accountability for the mediocrity of my lectures, that's what it too often means.

Freedom of the pulpit? Do I need it when preaching is mellifluous repetition of the sweet, conventional clichés of yesterday, sugarcoated with pop psychology to make them go down easier?

Freedom? Surrounded by our burglar alarms and medicine cabinets, our fears—heart attack, impotency, insanity, insolvency—this is freedom?

We Americans have built a society that has given an unprecedented measure of freedom to its citizens. I am given maximum space aggressively to pursue what I want, as long as I don't bump into you while you are getting yours. What we call culture is a vast supermarket of desire where citizens are treated as little more than self-interested consumers. I've got freedom of choice, but now what do I choose? We are free, but also terribly lonely, terribly driven. The nine-to-five job, monthly mortgage payments, overprogramed kids, dog-eat-dog contest for grades at the university—this is our freedom.

You see, *there is freedom, and then there is freedom.* And our problem, in this matter of freedom, is that *we may not even know what true freedom is.*

The book of Acts tells wonderful stories. Luke, master artist, tells a story, then lets you make up your own mind. Today's lesson from Acts tells some stories about people who were in bondage and people who were free. Listen and tell me who in this story is free.

[Read Acts 16:16–34.]

Paul and Silas were going to church one day and were accosted by a slave girl. Because this girl could tell people's fortunes, her owners made lots of money hiring her out to read palms and provide entertainment at business conventions. She was possessed by a demon (mentally unbalanced, we would say). She took to following Paul and Silas around, shouting at them, saying things about them.

Here is a picture of enslavement. If you have suffered through the torment of mental illness, if someone whom you love is in the grip of schizophrenia or terrible depression, you could tell us about bondage. It is as if something has you, something you can't shake, some dark, uncontrollable force which you are powerless to hold back.

Paul has enough of the young woman's raving and, in the name of Christ, cures her. Thank God, she is free!

But no, she is not free, because she is a slave, someone who is not a person but a piece of property, owned by someone else. And some of you, back in your own roots and family trees, had great-grandparents who were bought and sold. A slave. Can there be a more vivid image of human bondage?

Luke says, "When her owners saw that their hope of gain was gone, they seized Paul and Silas and dragged them into the market place before the rulers." Let's hear it for the business community!

One day Jesus healed a mentally deranged man by casting his demons into some swine (Luke 8:33). For this act of charity, Jesus was promptly escorted out of town by the local Pork Dealers Association.

Later, at a place called Ephesus, Paul had a big revival and many were converted and it was all wonderful— except for the members of Local 184 of the International Brotherhood of Artisans of Silver Shrines to Artemis. They didn't like it at all.

A student of mine at the divinity school led a crusade of his church to clean up his community. Good! Clean up the town, get out the dirty books and the beer joints, make it a better place for children and families. No, bad. How was he to know that one of his prominent church members owned the convenience store on the corner across from the high school?

My friend John Killinger, pastor of Lynchburg's First Presbyterian, will preach here next fall. In a sermon, John criticized Jerry Falwell. None of his church members attended Falwell's church and none of them agreed with his theology but, to John's chagrin, he learned on Monday morning how many of his church members had loaned Liberty Baptist money or had large accounts with Falwell enterprises.

Here is a young woman, chained her whole life to the hell of mental illness, and she is free. There ought to be rejoicing. But no, her owners are not free to do that. It was fine to give a dollar to the Mental Health Association drive last fall, but this is another matter. Religion has somehow gotten mixed up with economics here, and so her owners do what the vested ones always do when their interests are threatened.

Oh, we don't come right out and say that God is interfering with our business. We're not so dumb. No, we hire a public-relations firm that teaches us how to talk in front of a camera and how to answer reporters and put a good face on the corporation.

You have seen the ads: "Gee, Dad, I'm going to work for 'X' chemical company (you know the company, Dad—the one that made napalm back in Vietnam days) and I'm going to get to grow food to feed hungry people."

And the girl's owners say, "Judge, we're not against a little religion, as long as it is kept in its place. But these Jews are disturbing our city. They advocate customs which it is not lawful for us Romans to accept or practice."

No, we don't come right out and say that our financial self-interest is threatened; we say that our nation is threatened. "These missionaries are foreigners." Buy American!

Besides, they are Jews. And we all know what they are like. Money-grabbing, materialistic.

And if the nationalism and the anti-Semitism don't work, we'll throw in an appeal for old-time religion, saying, "They advocate customs that it is not lawful for us to practice." Nation, race, tradition—all stepping into line behind the dollar.

Then the crowd (democracy in action) falls into line behind the town's business leaders. They attack and beat Paul and Silas.

Paul and Silas are put into the back cell of the town prison, and the jailer locks them in the stocks. The liberators have become the imprisoned. Jesus has helped set a pitiful young woman free, but two of Jesus' people get jailed in the process.

The one who came preaching, "You will know the truth, and the truth will make you free," well, you know where he ended up.

So Paul and Silas end up in prison, languishing there. No, that's not the way the story goes. The story says, "About midnight Paul and Silas were praying and singing hymns to God, and the prisoners were listening to them . . ." Wait, these men in chains, legs locked in the stocks, are singing, praying, having some kind of a rally, there, in jail?

A few years ago, we were honored with a visit by Bishop Emilio de Carvalho, Methodist Bishop of Angola. What is it like to be the church in a Marxist country? we wanted to know. Is the new Marxist government supportive of the church? we asked.

"No," the bishop responded, "but we don't ask it to be supportive."

"Have there been tensions?" we asked.

"Yes," said the bishop. "Not long ago the government decreed that we should disband all women's organizations in the church.

"Oh, the women kept meeting. The government is not yet strong enough to do much about it."

"But what will you do when the government becomes stronger?"

"Well," he said, "we shall keep meeting. The government does what it needs to do. The church does what it needs to do. If we go to jail for being the church, we shall go to jail. Jail is a wonderful place for Christian evangelism. Our church made some of its most dramatic gains during the revolution when so many of us were in jail. In jail, you have everyone there, in one place. You have time to preach and teach. Sure, twenty of our Methodist pastors were killed during the revolution, but we came out of jail a much larger and stronger church."

And, as if seeing the drift of our questions, Bishop Carvalho said, "Don't worry about the church in Angola; God is doing fine by us. Frankly, I would find it much more difficult to be a pastor in Evanston, Illinois. Here, there is so much, so many things, it must be hard to be the church here."

The earth heaves, the prison shakes, the doors fly open, and everyone's chains fall off. The jailer wakes, and when he sees that the doors are open, is horrified. Knowing what happens to jailers who permit their prisoners to escape, he draws his sword and prepares to do the honorable thing for disgraced jailers. (Just having the key to someone else's cell doesn't make you free. Iron bars do not make a prison.)

Paul shouts, "Don't do it! We're all here, just singing."

The jailer says, "But you were bound in chains; now you were free to escape."

Paul says, "No, we prisoners are free to stay and you, our jailer, are chained to your sword, but now you can be free to escape."

And the jailer asks, "What do I have to do to be saved? What do I have to do to be free?" And he was baptized.

What is freedom? By the end of Luke's story, everyone who at first appeared to be free—the girl's owners, the judges, the jailer—are shown to be slaves. And everyone who first appeared to be enslaved—the poor girl, Paul, and Silas—are free.

Jesus does things like that to people.

Who pulls your strings?

Speaking at a conference on women in the church, someone rose and said, "The federal government has done more for the cause of women in this country than the church ever thought about. At last, because of government help, women are enabled to be on an equal level with men in the workplace."

And I had just heard, on the radio, that for the first time in history, the percentage of lung cancer among women who smoke is nearly as high as it is among men. The rate of hypertension, heart disease, and other stress-related diseases is climbing among women, and some feel that, in not too many years, the lifespan of the average American women will have shrunk to that of the average American man.

You've come a long way, to get where you got to today?

There is freedom and then there is freedom.

Earlier, Jesus had said, "If you continue in my word, you are truly my disciples, and you will know the truth, and the truth will make you free" (John 8:31–32).

They stiffened their necks, held their heads high, and answered, "What is this 'will make you free' business? We are descendants of Abraham, and have never been in bondage to anyone. How is that you say, 'You will be made free'?"

They lied. The ones who spoke so pridefully of their freedom spoke with the heel of Caesar upon their necks, slaves of Egypt, Assyria, Babylonia, and now Rome, anybody big enough to raise an army and blow through town. In truth, they were not free. Their boasts of freedom were but the rattling of their chains.

And Jesus said, "If the Son makes you free, you will be free" (John 8:36).

Dear Will:

I think this is just a wonderful sermon. I say that because one of the temptations of using this format is that it appears that if I am to comment, the comment will always be critical. I don't think that's appropriate, as sometimes I will not have anything critical to say but rather will want only to place the sermon within certain kinds of theological themes.

For example, I think what is so remarkable about this sermon is that it's an exercise in what Hans Frei and George Lindbeck are trying to do in their theological proposals showing how theology is an exercise in intratextuality. What you've tried to do by starting with our presumptions about freedom in America is to show how our presumptions make it very hard for us to read our lives through a text such as Acts. It's hard for us to read our lives biblically because we believe that we've already gotten the freedom you identify with Paul and Silas. Of course, we confuse freedom of choice with freedom of the spirit. It would be tempting for me, then, to engage in an extensive political theory lecture about how liberal presuppositions about the nature of the state and its governance always result in a subtle form of slavery.

One could pull out a little Foucault and show how modern enlightenment views have led to more profound forms of supervision on the part of the powers that be. You could do that, but I'm glad you didn't. You employed more immediate images that help us juxtapose our lives and the lives of Paul and Silas. Yet at the same time I think it's useful for me to point out that these theoretical issues are not unimportant. They inform us about the kinds of slavery we now find ourselves in and which we are tempted to call freedom. George Bernard Shaw somewhere said that Hell is where we have to do what we want to do, and in America we call that the land of the free.

One of the issues that you might have thought through more fully, however, is how the political understanding of freedom relates to the economic understanding. You nicely note how the background of the text really involves economic matters. However, you don't really develop that, and by the end of the sermon you are dealing more with political freedom. Of course, it is the case that one should not distinguish too strongly between these two, as it's only a capitalist economy that wants you to believe that there is some strong distinction between economic and political freedoms. However, you might have developed the economic issue a bit more by suggesting how we have subjected our political world in this country to supporting those with economic power and then we convince those without economic power that it is in their interest to have a politics determined by capitalist interests.

Indeed, in that respect I thought that one of the missing theological resources was the whole question of sin. You should have noted that when the slave girl's owners were confronted by the gospel, Paul and Silas were thrown in jail, because none of us want our sin exposed. So to talk about economic interest is another way of talking about sin. But sin adds a new dimension to the text, as it helps us see that we are gripped by powers from which we cannot be freed unless we are offered a new alternative. The call to repent and be baptized is not just a call to individual conversion, but to be part of a whole new set of practices embodied in a concrete people that give me an alternative to the world.

In that respect I thought one of the things that you might have done in terms of using the jail motif that the end of your sermon relies on so heavily was to develop the theme that Christian freedom finally derives from the fact that our enemies cannot determine the meaning of our dying. I was moved by your appeal to Bishop Emilio de Carvalho's story about the church in Angola.

What was so remarkable about his and their courage is that the notion that twenty Methodist pastors were killed during the revolution is, of course, horrible; but more horrible would be the loss of a church that knew how to remember them as saints. To be able to remember them as saints means that those who killed them cannot determine the meaning of their death.

This is where the issue of George Lindbeck's "intratextuality" becomes powerful. Christians are living a different story from that of their oppressors. Therefore the deaths we die in that story are not the deaths that those who would kill us think they are imposing on us. The reason that Paul and Silas remain free, even in chains, is because they know that the story that has grasped their lives is true. So what we have in this text from Acts is a complete revisioning of the world in which you nicely note that all who seem to have power and freedom in fact are enslaved by it, and those who do not are in fact free. I think the issue of the meaning of our deaths is important because that might let you say a bit more than you do in the sermon about how Jesus provides the context for Paul and Silas to be free while the jailer continues to be dependent on the sword.

One small exegetical issue that you might have considered a bit more in your sermon: Why was Paul irritated that the young woman who was possessed by a demon was following him and Silas around suggesting that they were truly servants of the most high God? She certainly had them right. It's always better to have some advertising; so why was Paul irritated? I think to suggest that she was mentally ill may be anachronistic. The scripture says that she was possessed by a spirit of divination, which may mean she was not mentally ill but really had a spirit. I suspect that the reason Paul did what he did is that it was a Pauline thing to do—namely, that he was part of a new world in which those spirits no longer had power. So you might have contrasted Paul's freeing her from that power to the kind of possession that captured the jailer.

I am impressed by how you have said better all the kinds of things that would take me a long time to say through the use of my more theoretical apparatus about the relationship between freedom and power. It has been one of the insights of contemporary social and political theory, especially that identified with Foucault and Derrida, that the forms of liberation in modernity are but more determinative forms of oppression exactly because we do not notice that they are oppression. For example, Foucault has so nicely seen how our fear of death makes us all subject to the power of modern medicine exactly because we think we are denying our fate through the power medicine gives. Ironically we just come under the power of physicians.

What I find so wonderful is how you have found a way to elicit that through the images provided in the sermon without getting into theoretical discussion. All of which is to say that it gives me pause about the relation between theory and sermonic form. I think that the sermonic form may well be the better argument.

Peace,

Stanley

CHAPTER TWO

Living Sacrifice

Opening Sunday
Thirteenth Sunday after Pentecost
Romans 12:1–8

"By the mercies of God, . . . present your bodies
as a living sacrifice, holy and acceptable to
God, which is your spiritual worship. Do not
be conformed to this world but be transformed
by the renewal of your mind."

I had this man in my last church who frequently greeted me at the end of the service by thrusting into my hand some newspaper article, usually from the *Wall Street Journal,* which he thought would be of help in his never-ending battle to educate his preacher.

One Sunday, he gave me an article by a national columnist, in which the columnist described how a young woman had been indicted in Chicago after her baby was found to have died from complications brought on by malnutrition and infection from rat bites. Why give me such an article? I found out at the end, when the columnist said, "I wish these preachers, who are always talking about what ought to be done on issues like abortion, would get out of their ivory towers and into the *real* world. Then they might see things differently."

You have heard this argument before, not only applied to preachers, but to Christians in general. The argument goes that if we Christians could only learn to accept the "real world" and "face facts," we would see things differently.

But such a demand of Christians begs the real question: Where is this "real world" to which we are to adjust? Who defines what is real? Is the "real world" one in which a baby dies in a Chicago tenement house from malnutrition and rat bites? Is that the world to which we are to adjust?

At the beginning of this summer we saw the film *Crazy People*. It isn't that great a movie, but its thesis is very funny. It tells about inmates of a mental hospital who, through a strange turn of events, are given high-paying jobs in the advertising industry because, being crazy, they know no better than to write advertisements that tell the truth! One of the advertisements reads, "We know you love him, but if he dies, wouldn't you like to have $100,000 and a Mercedes-Benz? John Hancock Life Insurance." The American public, having been told lies for so long, hears these truthful advertisements as something strange and wonderful.

In such a world, when we gather, despite the beautiful music and the charming building, there will be an inevitable hard edge to what we do here. It is the tension of confrontation, the experience of being caught in the cross fire of a debate over what is real.

"By the mercies of God, . . . present your bodies as a living sacrifice, holy and acceptable to God, which is your spiritual worship. Do not be conformed to this world but be transformed by the renewal of your mind."

"Present yourselves as a living sacrifice . . . . Do not be conformed to this world but be transformed." There is our text. Right up front, on Opening Sunday, let's be honest and admit that we are all gathered here in the

Chapel today to engage in a debate over what is real, what is normal.

This is not some course in the Department of Religion in which we spend the semester talking about religion as sociology, anthropology, or history, the truth of which makes no difference because nobody in the class will make a decision about truth anyway.

I'll be more honest. I am here this morning, and most other Sundays, to convert you, to take as my modest aim, by the end of the service, to get you upon that altar up there, to invite you to make a "sacrifice" of yourself, not by putting a dollar in the plate, but by putting your body up on that altar—in short, to get you to worship.

Of course, the rest of the university also wants to convert you. The only difference is, like Walter Mondale in the presidential debate, I will tell you what I plan to do, whereas most of the rest of the university, like Ronald Reagan, won't tell you. We bring you here to the university, put you through various courses, and tell you that we don't want "to force anything down your throats"; rather, we want you to "make up your own mind." Yet the educational philosophy that encourages people to "make up their own minds" *is* a philosophy. It assumes that the most important aspect of truth is not whether or not it actually happens to be true, but whether or not you personally feel it to be true.

My point is that most of your work here at the university proceeds from a philosophical standpoint, some assumption about what is true and good. The trouble is that most of our work here proceeds without any admission of what those philosophical assumptions are. We are busy putting the make on you, converting you into a philosophy of life, all the while telling you that we want you to "think for yourself" and "make up your own minds," which is itself a philosophy of life.

One reason we don't recognize that the university operates out of a set of philosophical assumptions is that most of us have already been converted into these assumptions, even without having to pay tuition and come to a university. Our university at its worst is no more than a mirror of our culture as it already is. The prevailing understanding of our culture as it is, is that the individual, in his or her autonomy, individuality, and detachment is the sole center of all meaning.

Hannah Arendt noted that the modern secular world destroyed God, the family, and community, throwing people, not out into the world, but merely back upon ourselves. All we are left with is a sovereign individual with little source of meaning in life other than the individual. This is a lonely way to go. Is that why the Greek word for the self, *id,* which Freud coined to describe ourselves at our most significant, is, paradoxically, the root for our word idiot? Left only to ourselves, there is very little self.

Against this corrupted consciousness of the modern world, the church launches its Sunday assault. To be here in the Chapel is to find one's modern little self caught in the cross fire between two competing and quite conflicting definitions of normality.

Against our self-assured, conventional, socially acceptable definitions of normality, in coming to this Chapel we expose ourselves to a devastating power, devastating simply because it is true while other powers are not. We are talking about God. It is a power that can be described best only through poetry. Today's psalm, Psalm 114:

> *The sea looked and fled,*
> *Jordan turned back.*
> *The mountains skipped like rams,*
> *the hills like lambs.*

What ails you, O sea, that you flee?
O Jordan, that you turn back? . . .
Tremble, O earth, at the presence of the Lord,
  at the presence of the God of Jacob,
who turns the rock into a pool of water.

It is by this same power that a powerless young Jew set the world of abnormality on its ear. Confronted by the pretentious power of the state, he said, "Render to Caesar the things that are Caesar's, and to God the things that are God's." Before the self-serving spirit of a world come of age, he countered, "If you would find your life, you must first lose it." And then he proceeded to go about in such a disconcertingly normal way— healing those who were ill, telling truth, feeding the hungry, raising the dead, stampeding swine—that systemic abnormality simply had to put him away, as it thought, for keeps. For a time it seemed as if "the facts of life" had won, namely, that death had triumphed. And yet, among his paralyzed followers, clinging only to themselves around a simple table, he returned in power, having walked into the jaws of abnormality, having pulled its teeth, having subverted the old order.

When the power of life appears in this Jew from Nazareth, systemic abnormality, to which we are always in danger of becoming accustomed, is thrown into disarray.

This is the power let loose here on Sunday morning, when we are at our best. It is the power that summons every one of us to submit to transformation. In the Sunday presence of this power, our fingers are one by one pulled loose from their tight grip on the status quo and we are wrenched away from the world as it is.

I know a junior, a Presbyterian. In Michigan, he says, he never thought much about being a Presbyterian. But he came to Duke and, for the first time in his little Presbyterian life, he was forced to explain himself.

"Why do you get up and go to church on Sunday morning?" they asked.

"What makes you think you're so much better than everybody else?" someone asked.

It was a new experience for him, being odd, peculiar. Back in Grand Rapids, it was normal to be a Presbyterian. Here, he's abnormal.

The usual question asked of Christians by abnormality is, Will it work? That is, is this course practical, reasonable, possible, and above all, can this be had without cost?

To those who have been ravished by divine normality, the questions raised by the world's abnormality are quite beside the point. We have not gathered primarily to "address the issues" as the world has identified them, but rather to upend and subvert terrestrial abnormality, which maims and kills everything it touches. Christ did not offer better answers to the social, religious, and political issues of his time or ours. Rather, he trampled death, the supreme Lord of Abnormality, and gave life to those entombed, death always being the first choice of abnormality, every time our race has had a chance to choose.

As Aidan Kavanagh has said, we have demonstrated that there is virtually nothing that we will not transmute into life's antithesis. Food to weapons, aid into coercion, justice into terrorism, love into libido, liberation into tyranny, education into rationalization. In the church's two-thousand-year pilgrimage, we have learned that all the money, power, and good intentions that systemic abnormality musters can never change this viciousness into virtue, abnormality into normality. Nor can we by our own efforts. Systemic abnormality has a hideous strength, and it is dangerous to underestimate its power to eat one alive. (Thanks to Aidan Kavanagh, *On Liturgical Theology* [Pueblo Publishing Co.,

New York, 1984], pp. 174–175 for his thoughts on the "normality" of Sunday worship.)

Thus Paul urges us to "not be conformed to this world but be transformed by the renewal of your mind." Thus this Sunday morning I have beckoned you to come away, to stand apart, to look odd, abnormal, for the supreme purpose that you may be embraced by divine normality. True normality can only be restored when we are given eyes to see what is, and when we offer ourselves to it.

And thus Paul urges, "By the mercies of God, . . . present your bodies as a living sacrifice, holy and acceptable to God, which is your spiritual worship."

Having nursed on abnormality for so long, there is no way for us to be weaned except by drastic alteration of minds and hearts so that reality is perceived in new and unforgettable ways. Transformation occurs when we are addressed by something that offers us a way to give up ourselves so that we might find ourselves. Churchill calls for blood, sweat, and tears in adversity. Martin Luther King, Jr., tells of a dream. Bach sets faith to music so that the inscrutable Holy One enters our midst and embraces us. Minds are changed when imaginations are freed by giving human emotion a massive dose of normality. There is nothing easy about it. It takes hard work, weekly, every Sunday work, yes, and suffering. It costs lives. Sunday is dangerous.

Is that why Paul uses the image of *sacrifice*? The word conjures up screaming animals before stone altars, blood trickling down marble steps, and the raised, flashing knife of the priest preparing to slit the throat of some bleating beast.

And that, Paul says, is at the heart of being a Christian. Nobody comes to God without cost. That "sacrifice" being laid upon the bloody altar of God is *you*.

"Unlike a lot of people on this campus, I don't drink," he said to me. "You see, I am planning on going to medical school. Therefore I must make the best grades I can. I need all my brain cells in good working order. Alcohol destroys brain cells. Therefore I don't drink."

And that is one basis for morality.

But here the motivation for right living, *orthopraxy,* flows from right worship, *orthodoxy.* How we live on this campus, Monday through Saturday, flows from how we have worshipped here on Sunday, from this collision in which we have participated, this collision between abnormality and normality, between true and false.

So Paul urges the church to be more than simply good. "By the mercies of God, present yourselves as living sacrifice; this is your true worship. Do not be conformed to this world but be transformed by the renewal of your mind."

Here is reality, to lay ourselves on that altar. That is why we have such a large altar, one so big that it takes four football players to move it. It has to be big to get so many of you on it.

For the hard truth is not IF you will give your life, but TO WHOM you will give it! Many of us are offering up ourselves on lesser altars, before smaller gods.

I know a sophomore. Came here last year all buttoned down, sure of himself. Your average, high-SAT-scoring, hyperachieving freshman. He got turned upside down, inside out one evening here at the Chapel. Messed him up for good, as far as I can tell. Gave up a sophomore summer in Vail or Los Alamos to build houses for poor people in Americus, Georgia.

To most of the rest of the campus, that's called odd. Here in the Chapel, we call it normal.

In the words of an Anglican Communion prayer, "Here we offer and present unto thee, O Lord, our selves, our souls and bodies, to be a reasonable, holy, and living sacrifice unto thee." Amen.

Dear Will:

I thought your opening sermon for the school year was challenging and truthful. One of the reasons I thought the sermon was so good is that I heard a bit of myself in it. I loved that part about making up their own minds because that's a theme I've been developing lately, ever since I saw *Dead Poets Society.* I thought you could have done more with it. The freshmen really don't understand yet that they have come here to make up their own minds, as they think they've come here to learn a lot of stuff that will put them on the power trails of the American society. That's why you needed to do a bit more about how universities are committed to making autonomous citizens for democracies. In other words, universities are not communities that are ends in themselves in our society, but rather serve the political purposes, or at least ideologies, of capitalist and liberal democratic social orders. As a result, universities are really not independent or autonomous institutions, because we promise parents that we will send their children back to them just about the way they sent them to us— that is, as liberal democratic capitalists.

It would be fun to think of Duke as a Marxist university. Could we survive as a Marxist university? What if we were a Christian university who sent kids back to their parents at least as screwed up as Marxists would make them? That would give your sermon a bit more bite, I think. This would show how radical is your claim that the church stand apart from the university in terms of the kind of conversion you are trying to effect in the Chapel as opposed to the conversion of university.

Of course in that is the whole ambiguity of the Chapel at this university. After all, you and I are faithful servants of the university and the university is not going to keep us around if we say things that are ultimately going to be antithetical to what the university wants to be about. It seems to me you might acknowledge honestly that it's not at all clear if this university Chapel is the church. It's not clear because it's not clear who is the master here. However, as a minister of the gospel charged by the United Methodist Church to preach honestly, you have to preach what you know to be true whether the university Chapel is church or not. Insofar as you preach truthfully, then the Chapel becomes church. I've always thought that you might need to be a bit more reflective in some of your sermons about the ambiguous character of the Chapel. It would be a useful theological lesson for most of the people who come to the Chapel, even though it would be quite painful, particularly for you and me.

I thought the major theological issue in the sermon was your use of sacrificial language following the Pauline text. The language is unavoidable, and you were quite right to use it, but I don't think you used it well. The problem with your use of sacrificial language was that it had an inherent individualistic cast. Even the examples you used were about individuals. For example, the sophomore who went to Habitat for Humanity. What is missing in that example is a sense of how the whole church is God's sacrifice as the body of Christ. After all, the church is the continuation of Christ's cross through Jesus' resurrection and the giving of the Spirit. We are God's presence in the world now so that the world might know that God refuses to let our rejection, our violence, determine God's relationship with God's creation. The whole church becomes the sacrifice.

Your appeal to the altar was just right, but you needed explicitly to associate the altar with the Eucharistic sacrifice. We see how we are misled in our sermons when we do not follow the sermon with the Eucharist. You've done so well in helping some in the chapel recover a sense of the importance of the Eucharist, but when it's not practiced as the whole body there, then you tend to lose it as central for your own homiletical practice. In the Eucharist we see that the sacrifice is not something *we* do but that the eucharistic celebration is *God's* great good news that God has made us part of God's kingdom and thus part of Christ's cross. It is not that we are making the sacrifices, but that God is making us holy so we might be capable of witnessing to the world the kind of God that sacrifices for the world.

The feminist critique of the idea of sacrifice seems to me to be exactly right. Feminists point out that people like Reinhold Niebuhr who made self-sacrifice into a norm in and of itself were inherently destructive to women. Oddly enough, Niebuhr's account of sacrifice was abstract and separated from the cross. For him the notion of self-sacrifice was a principle in and of itself that Christ's cross exemplified. That is not appropriate to the way Christians are taught to think about the sacrifice of Christ. Christ, as John Howard Yoder always emphasizes, was not about sacrificing as a good in and of itself, but rather Christ's cross is what one would expect for One who is at once the preacher and the embodiment of God's kingdom. Christ got put to death for reminding the world that God is our ruler. What is at stake here is to call into question certain satisfaction theories of the atonement that are correlative to a church that is socially accommodated. Sacrifice becomes a big thing where there are people who no longer feel themselves in fundamental conflict with the world.

I thought your use of the bloody altar was just right, but you need to be honest and say that even though we believe the church has replaced that altar, it remains damn bloody. That is why sacrifice is still needed. The script in which you put sacrifice can easily be a humanistic one, that in order to do good in the world we need to subordinate our own interests to those greater goods.

This sacrifice of God that we find in the cross isn't just about doing good, but about relieving the world of its necessity to violence. I thought there you could really connect the issue of sacrifice and reality by suggesting how our world, at its most real, is created to be nonviolent. For nothing is more real than the eucharistic celebration that celebrates God's union with us redeeming the world from its violence.

In an interesting way you might have taken up the theme that the church as God's sacrifice means the end of all the bloody sacrifices the world feels the need to make. We no longer need to sacrifice animals on the altar because God has made the ultimate sacrifice in Christ. We no longer need to sacrifice one another through our wars, trying to assure ourselves that the goods of the nation are real, because now God has ended those sacrifices, helping us know that only God can claim our lives. Christian nonviolence is built on the presumption not that there is nothing worth dying for, but rather that God alone has the right to command our lives. When you take that tack it seems to me the bodily, both physically and communally, aspect of sacrifice cannot be avoided. That's a real challenge to the individualism of our culture.

I make these points while wondering how in the world you could develop these themes and still have the existential power that the sermon evoked? Your examples were wonderful, and I have no examples to offer you to develop these theological themes. So I have the sneaking suspicion that if you had preached the sermon along the lines I'm suggesting, it would have been a poorer sermon. These are not easy matters, but I guess that's the reason why it's important that we need one another.

Thanks for being such a wonderful friend.

Peace,

Stanley

CHAPTER THREE

Be Imitators of Me

Eighteenth Sunday after Pentecost
Philippians 3:17–21

A seminarian made an appointment with me and asked me if I would take him on for an independent study course.

What do you want to study? "Preaching," he said. "I want to do an independent study course with you in preaching."

"OK. What do you want to study about preaching?" I asked.

"I want to learn how to preach like you," he said.

"That's ridiculous," I said. "You can't imitate me. For one thing, you're from Iowa. To preach the way I preach, you'd have to be born in South Carolina, somewhere between Greenville and Columbia. You can't preach the way I preach. Besides, I don't want you to be my disciple, to imitate me."

Reflecting on that conversation, I realize that my reluctance to have that young man sign on with me had nothing to do with modesty, a virtue with which I am not overly endowed. It had to do with my discomfort at having a young person looking over my shoulder, patterning his way after my way. I don't want that responsibility. Besides, the way I do it could be wrong. And I'd rather not have my errors reflected in the life of someone else. (Those of you who are teachers know what I mean.)

But then we come to today's peculiar text. Saint Paul in one of his more unguarded moments?

"Be imitators of me," says Paul. "You have an example in us." And this was no slip of the Pauline tongue. Paul gives exactly the same advice to the Corinthians, Thessalonians, and Galatians. "Become as I am," he tells them. Is there no limit to apostolic presumption?

I'd like to know who are these "enemies of the cross" whose "god is the belly." Who is Paul talking about here? Sensualists, libertines? "Their God is the belly." Sounds like a description of the inhabitants of fraternity row or Thursday's *Chronicle* editorial.

"Their God is the belly"? We don't know. Something in their life-style bothered Paul. *What we do know is that Paul unashamedly offered his own life-style to counter theirs. "Join in imitating me."*

Picture this: I begin a class by saying, "Class, this is a course in homiletics. The goal of this course is to see how well all of you can imitate me."

It's one thing to take a course where most of the assigned readings are textbooks written by the professor, but this is too much. It strikes us as the height of conceit—imitate me!

No. What I say is: "Class, I'm going to lay out a few principles for you, a few interesting (though not my own) ideas, some insights for discussion; then I want you to make up your own mind. You see, I respect your identity, your individuality. I don't want to force myself on you or, God forbid, make you disciples of me. *I'm not like Paul.*"

That's what I say. And I will tell you that I do it because I'm appropriately self-effacing, modest, respectful of your personal freedom to be whatever it is you personally decide to be.

Translated into honest English, this means: I want to get through this class without taking responsibility for you. My goal is to trot you through the university in such a fashion that you will be as much a stranger to me on the day of your graduation as when you arrived. We live in a lonely society based upon the Constitution, which created the individual, an entity unknown until the Enlightenment—the individual who is a bundle of individual rights, individual opinions, individual claims. Our society puts more stress on individual freedom and individual rights than any ever known.

Unfortunately, loneliness is an unavoidable by-product of a culture that believes that guarding individual prerogatives is more important than fostering community. My society gives me maximum space to exercise my "rights," but gives me no help in deciding which rights are worth having. This culture makes me free, but then is unable to tell me what is worth doing with my freedom. And in a church, a university, corrupted by that society, everyone becomes a stranger. I say that I want community, but wouldn't want to pay the price required to relinquish my individual space. So most of us say, "Stay out of my life and I'll stay out of yours."

A few years ago, one of the biggest gripes of our students was lack of enforcement of the noise policy. Students demanded that someone come to the dorm to tell offenders to turn their stereos down. A dean asked,

"Well, why don't you simply walk next door and ask the person to turn the volume down, tell him that it's bothering people?"

"Look. That's not my business. If I tell him something like that, he may criticize something I'm doing, and then where would we be?"

I'm not picking on students. At a faculty retreat a few years ago, one of my colleagues asked, "Does it bother you that some of our students are sexually promiscuous, that some of them are indulging in self-destructive behavior and addictive practices?"

Well, we said, we must respect their privacy. They're all adults. We're not their mothers. (What we mean is, God forbid that we should hold our students accountable not only for what they *know* but for who they *are* because, if we did that, then you know what might happen? Students might turn and hold US accountable, speak the truth to us about OUR life-style and personal habits and inconsistencies, and *then where would we be?*)

See? Students HAVE joined in imitating us faculty after all! The Office of Student Affairs is asking for it, telling students that it's not good for their academics for them to be drunk Friday through Sunday. You tell students that, then some student will turn on us faculty and ask us what we were doing Friday through Sunday, and then where would we be? You criticize some student for being unprepared on Monday and next thing you know students will be challenging us for being unprepared in class, and then where would we be?

On our way to a rediscovery of the etymology of the word "college," a collection of colleagues with a common purpose.

A Duke senior, recently returned from a year at Oxford, told me that one of his regrets was that he had just sort of drifted through this place, taking this course or that one, not really giving his best, sometimes faking it, not really engaged. No one had looked over his shoulder while he was busy taking this and taking that. No one had taken the trouble to get to know him well enough to know when he was faking. He envied the "moral tutor" tradition at Oxford. Education, at its deepest, is a form of imitation.

Paul, in appealing to his flock for imitation, placed himself squarely within that moral and pedagogical tradition that assumed that a teacher is one who is willing to be exposed to the imitative glare of a student, which asserted that the purpose of learning is imitation of a master, that teachers have a responsibility to live as they teach, to walk as they speak, and that pupils are challenged not only to know about some things but also to be transformed by someone. (See Fred Craddock, *Philippians* [Atlanta: John Knox Press, 1987], pp. 64–69.)

In the European Enlightenment, with the creation of the individual, morality was re-created into something available to everybody. Anybody could be good by simply thinking clearly, using Kantian reason, common sense, or other individualistic, natural endowments, which were alleged to reside in everybody, democratically bestowed, regardless of that person's upbringing or social status.

This view of goodness was counter to that offered by moralists like Aristotle, who taught that goodness was not a matter of being "reasonable," of making "right" choices—rather, goodness was a matter of being a good person, being someone who had been trained to be good. You must be taught to be good. Aristotle's chief analogy for morality was learning how to ride a horse. You can't learn to ride a horse by reading a book. You learn to ride a horse by watching someone else who is good at it, by being led step by step by that person, by imitating the moves, coaxed into it, criticized, guided, until those moves, the feel of the reins, become yours.

Here was an unabashedly "elitist" view of morality. Aristotle, unlike Kant, believed that morality was not something available to everyone as a natural endowment. Morality belonged to that aristocracy who had taken the time and the trouble to become better persons than they would have been if left to their own devices. Goodness was more than a matter of *knowing* good. It was a matter of *being* good, having the moves and the skills that morality requires.

As Martin Luther noted, you don't get apples from a thornbush. You get apples from an apple tree. You get good works from good people.

But away from Aristotle and back to Jesus. For Jesus, being good was not an intellectual problem of knowing what I ought to do in this situation—ethics in our day. As was sometimes said in the church in my part of the world, "You can't talk the talk if you don't walk the walk." Jesus unabashedly asked not just for agreement; he demanded discipleship—learning the moves, walking the walk, following him down the narrow path that he trod. Jesus asked for imitation. He wanted followers, not admirers.

Martin Luther King, Jr., didn't just admire Gandhi's nonviolent resistance. He imitated Gandhi.

For this little band of Christians at Philippi, constantly in danger of seduction by the majority pagan culture, there was no better textbook than the lives of those like Paul who bore the burden of leadership. Lifestyle is converted through life-style, and there is no weaseling out of the truth that discipleship is utterly dependent on our being able to identify examples, saints, people worthy of imitation. If we can't point to examples, even to ourselves, we have very little to say.

If every hundred years or so we cannot point to a Teresa of Calcutta, or a Martin Luther King, Jr., or a Desmond Tutu, we Christians have a problem, because the world is quite right in judging our religion by the sort of lives that it produces. Lacking changed lives, we pervert the gospel into an intellectual dilemma, some head trip, rather than a life-style trip. Being Christian is a matter of following someone who is headed somewhere I would not have gone if left to my own devices.

In my last parish, in the middle of a sermon on Lazarus and Dives, I read an account, out of a Brazilian newspaper, about how the poor of Brazil are now selling organs from their bodies to the rich. The story quoted a man named Walter who had recently sold his eyes to a rich person for corneal transplant. Walter, who has never had a job, was quoted as saying, "At last I can *see* my family to a better life."

I just read the story; that's all.

Next morning, Monday, when I arrived in my office the telephone was ringing. It was Debbie. Debbie was our resident congregational activist. She lived with her teacher husband in a small house near the church.

"I haven't slept all night," Debbie said.

"Why?" I asked.

"Because of Walter! I can't get him out of my mind. I got David up this morning at five o'clock. We talked. We prayed. We were going to get a new car. We can live without a new car. We were going to buy a new stereo. We don't need it. We are going to double our giving to the church if you can promise me that this money will go to help someone like Walter."

I thought to myself, I slept like a baby last night.

My fidelity as a disciple hangs by a slender thread of grace provided me by people like Debbie.

So go ahead. Imitate me. Demand that my miserable

49

little life be a worthy example. Do me a favor. Don't let me off the discipleship hook. Insist that I teach by the way I walk rather than merely by the book. Insist that there be a congruency between what I practice and what I profess.

Imitate me.

The bread was broken and the wine was poured for Communion. I stretched out my hands over the Table for the eucharistic prayer. A child on the first row was heard to say, "Look, Mommy, he's trying to look like Jesus."

It is not an inappropriate thing to say.

Dear Will:

Well, it's finally happened. I kept thinking you were going to preach a sermon in which my only response would be "Amen" and "Isn't that wonderful!" Of course, one of the reasons I'm so pleased with the sermon is it was material from my essays. I can't remember who said it, but it's been a working rule of thumb for theologians that if our theology finally doesn't preach, it can't be worth much. Therefore I am happy to hear my theology preached in a way that is so powerful. That Philippians text of Paul's was an invitation for you to develop some stuff that I had given you recently, and, by God, you did it wonderfully.

I think it's worthwhile to say how important the moral relationship is between us. We're not friends as an end in itself, but we're friends brought together by the common activity of trying to be faithful to God. That's why we don't need to worry about giving each other credit. I think a lot about the importance of anonymity. It first occurred to me when I heard a feminist criticizing the way men do theology because we always need to give it ownership. We put our name on it and we have to get tenure through it. In contrast, she suggested that women were working more communally, not feeling the need to claim ownership in that individualistic way. Whether she's right about women or not I don't know, but I know she's right about what it means to be Christians. We are not thinkers in some individualistic way, but rather we are trying to make a contribution to the upbuilding of an ongoing community and tradition. It is therefore my hope that when I hear my words in your sermons they are not my words or your words, but they are the words of all those who have preceded us that make it possible for such words finally to be God's words for the upbuilding of the Christian community. As I often tell my graduate students, creativity is forgetting where you read it. Finally it is about how we all depend on one another to live faithful to God's good work among us.

Interestingly enough, I think that has much to do with the theme of imitation in the sermon. Paul can say, Be imitators of me as I am of Christ. (By the way, I don't think that was an unguarded moment, but indeed that is the very heart of what Paul was about, as you indicated in your sermon.) John Schutz had a book on Paul that develops that in terms of the whole notion of authority in Paul. Paul could and should call attention to himself, because in doing so he thought it was calling attention to Christ. We Christians cannot avoid that. We must finally reflect Christ's life to one another if we are to know Christ at all.

That's a reminder of the Christology presuppositions behind the notion of imitation. Jesus is not an eternal possibility always available to all persons if they just make use of their experience. Jesus is only available through people whose lives have been touched by Christ. That is the inextricable historical character of our faith which must disci-

51

pline the language of grace. Of course, that is what has been behind my criticisms of some of your sermons that have been so gracious about grace.

The other thing that I thought was so wonderful about the sermon was how you reminded us that such imitation inextricably involves collegiality. That was a wonderful touch, to show that when teachers ask students to imitate them, it is a reminder that we are part of a college, which implies common purpose. So we are only able to ask for imitation as part of an ongoing enterprise which is for the upbuilding of the body.

The whole focus of the modern university is to deny the significance of the teacher for what is taught. In that respect I couldn't help personalizing what you were saying deeply. When I first began teaching, fresh from that Yale education you know so well, I tried to subordinate my personality to the subject. I thought the idea was to let the subject of Christian ethics be the primary actor in the classroom and I would simply try to be a mirror through which the students saw that. What a terrible teacher I was! You are quite right, such attempts at so-called objectivity were nothing but cowardice. I feared having students take me seriously because I didn't want to face the seriousness of what it was to be a teacher. Students soon made me better than I was, however, by forcing me to take myself seriously, since they took me seriously. There is simply no way to avoid that, though the contemporary university is built on the presumption that it can be avoided. As a result we are an institution of mammoth self-deception, since we cannot acknowledge the very process that makes us morally intelligible.

That is why the university so desperately needs the supporting institution of the church. Because imitation is so unavoidable as part of teaching, we need a more substantive community to stand against and judge those examples. If I did not have the church ultimately to stand over against me as teacher, I could not proceed. For without the Debbies, how could we ever trust the fact that we have been separated out to enjoy privileges as thinkers that would otherwise be unjustified?

The way you ended the sermon was wonderful. You asked us to hold you accountable and therefore to imitate you, but then you told that wonderful story of the little child suggesting in eucharistic celebration that you were trying to be like Jesus. That is to direct the attention exactly right, and you knew enough to know when to shut up. One of the things I so admire about your sermons is that you oftentimes let us make the connections. It's a hard discipline to allow that to happen, but you know, just as any good teacher knows, that often you don't want to say explicitly what you know because when you say it explicitly, it cannot be known by the learner in the way necessary for it to be known truthfully. I think that's the reason why stories like that are so crucial for the sermon, because the story doesn't say—it shows.

It's wonderful to be able to write in this vein as I really do feel like a brother.

Peace,

Stanley

CHAPTER FOUR

Ordinary People

Parents' Weekend
Twentieth Sunday after Pentecost
Ruth 1:1–19a

"Ruth said, 'Entreat me not to leave you . . . ;
for where you go I will go . . . ;
your people shall be my people,
and your God my God."

It's Parents' Weekend here and, through some act of divine serendipity, the lectionary has assigned as our first reading a passage from the book of Ruth.

The book of Ruth is a family story, an ancient novella whose origins may be three thousand years old. It's an old story, but I'm claiming that it's a true story because it's a story about a family in trouble. Here is a middle-class family that's hit on hard times and has to move, a father who dies leaving his wife and sons poorly provided for, two sons who marry women of another religion and race, a stepmother who doesn't understand her daughters-in-law yet finds herself linked to them in misery. It's a story about a family so beset with problems, and bills to pay, and children who won't do right, and tensions between a mother and daughters-in-law, ordinary people; in short, a family a great deal like yours, like mine.

Or am I doing a disservice to your family? It's Parents' Weekend, and there you sit with Mom and Dad. So perhaps your family doesn't have problems. That makes your family . . . unusual.

Our story, the story of Ruth, is about a more ordinary family, that is, a family where it's tough to be in the family and keep living and loving one another. An ordinary family.

A Duke student told me last week that her problem with Parents' Weekend was what to do with two sets of parents. They're staying at different motels. She's got to balance 50 percent of her weekend with her father and his new wife and the other 50 percent with her mother and her fiancé. It's complicated.

Last year, I told a Duke student how much I enjoyed meeting his mom as she left the Chapel after the service. "Did your dad not make it down this year?" I asked.

"Dad was busy," he said. Then he said, "No, that's not really true. Dad is on his second time through an alcohol treatment center, so he couldn't be here."

It's complicated to be in a family, especially an ordinary one.

Our story is set in the time of the Judges in Israel, when, according to the last verse of the book of Judges, there was an ineffective national administration and "every man did what was right in his own eyes" (Judg. 21:25). Violence in the streets, political intrigue, corruption in places high and low, in short, a tough time for marriage, tough on children, hard to be a family.

As if the moral chaos were not enough, there was economic disaster as well. There was "a famine in the land" (Ruth 1:1). Bloated bellies of little children, old people dying in the streets, vast wanderings of hungry beggars. Not a pretty sight.

Naomi and her husband leave their home in Bethlehem and travel to the wilds of Moab, hearing that things are better there. Have you ever been to Moab? It's a rough, out-of-the-way sort of place. You don't want to go down there unless you have to. Back in Genesis, after Abraham and Lot parted, Lot went up and lived in a cave with his two daughters (Lot's wife had been turned into a pillar of salt earlier, so Lot was fairly much on his own). At any rate, Lot's two daughters were unmarried. They noted that their father was getting old and their prospects for husbands were not good, so they got their father drunk, and while he was drunk they went in to him and . . . nine months later each had a son, by her own father. One son was named Moab, who became the "father of the Moabites" (Gen. 19:37).

(Parents, I know this is a Bible story you think inappropriate for your children, but I'm trying to explain why life among these Moabites was no picnic. You have to be really desperate, really hungry, to move your family to Moab.)

At any rate, Naomi and her husband are desperate. They take their sons and move to Moab. And, wouldn't you know it—no sooner have they unpacked than their sons are dating a couple of Moabite girls. Naomi is now a single parent. Her husband died as soon as they got to Moab. How she wishes her husband were there to help her deal with the problem of the boys' infatuation with these foreign women! But she's on her own, single parent. She does her best.

Naomi says, "Mahlon [her oldest son], it's not that What's-her-name is a bad girl . . . "

"Her name is Ruth, Mother . . . "

"All right, Ruth. It's not that Ruth is a bad girl, it's just that she has not had all the advantages that you have had. Her people have different values from our family. She's just a little . . . "

"What you're trying to say is she's a Moabite, right, Mother?" said Mahlon.

Well, Naomi gets about as far with this argument as some of you have with your sons and daughters in similar situations. Besides, where is Mahlon going to find a nice, middle-class, churchgoing girl out in Moab?

A few months later, Naomi has got herself two Moabite daughters-in-law.

She tries to make the best of it. "Dear," she says to Ruth one day, "you're so pretty, so naturally pretty, don't you think you can get along with just a tad less eyeliner? And, honey, I don't know that a low-cut gold lamé blouse is right for church."

It's tough being a mother-in-law!

But it gets a great deal tougher. Both of Naomi's sons die. And Naomi is left alone with two daughters-in-law whom she hardly even knows, much less likes.

After the death of her sons she says to the two girls, "Girls, I'm going back home to Bethlehem, back to my own people. I'm now a single woman, with no marketable skills, no prospect for another marriage, no future. I can't help you. You are young—go help yourselves. You don't need a dependent old woman like me around. Go on back to your people here in Moab."

What her daughters-in-law say surprises Naomi. "No. You are now our people. We will go with you."

Naomi tries to talk sense into them. "Look. You are women, unmarried women. We live in a patriarchal society—even though nobody knows that's what we're living in here in a few hundred years B.C., until the feminist movement tells us. Poor, unmarried, vulnerable women. You are Moabites. Stay here where there's some hope for you."

Orpah left, but Ruth clung to Naomi. (It's the same Old Testament word here that Genesis uses when it says of marriage that "a man cleaves to his wife, and they become one flesh," Gen. 2:24.) She clung to her, as if she were married. She refused to leave the old woman.

Naomi said, "Even if I get a husband in Bethlehem, I'm long past having children. I can have no more sons for you, my dear."

Ruth countered Naomi's pleadings with pleadings of her own, with one of the most beloved speeches in the Bible:

"Entreat me not to leave you or to return from following you; for where you go I will go . . . ; your people shall be my people, and your God my God; where you die I will die, and there will I be buried."

She's a Moabite. She's a single woman. It appears that Ruth has thrown her life away for nothing more than her mother-in-law.

When Abraham and Sarah were told to pick up and move to a strange land, God made a promise that he would bless them and be with them. But Ruth has no such divine reassurance. She links her life with Naomi on the basis of nothing more substantial than the affection one young woman has for an older one. It's a story about the strange yokings, the unusual linkages that occur in love in an ordinary family.

Yokings and linkages made all the more strange because you and I live in a culture that doesn't understand such clinging and claiming of one person by another. We have trouble understanding this story, not because it is over two thousand years old, but because we have constructed a society that acts as if it were possible to be a full human being with no attachments, no claims, no bonds between people. For us, the individual is everything, the free, autonomous, liberated, self-sufficient individual standing alone.

We have devised an educational system to suit our

ideology of the individual. Here we educate by detaching you from your family, moving you out of the home, putting you in the hands of strangers, abandoning you to your peer group, and after we have completely detached you from home, family, tradition, community, we give you a degree. We thereby imply that the way to wisdom is by making everyone a stranger to everyone else.

We are shocked whenever someone comes along who makes a claim on our lives—parents who have opinions about our behavior, children who hold parents accountable. We are shocked because we have defined freedom as the fewest possible number of attachments. Such "freedom" makes marriage, family, the bearing of children incomprehensible. After all, why would anybody want to limit his or her options by becoming unnecessarily tied down to the messy complications of other human beings?

Ironically, many of us are feeling anything but free. Parents, in a well-intentioned effort to "give our children freedom," abandon their children to the most tyrannical, totalitarian master of all—their own peers. Our old people perish in isolation and selfishness, stored in vast communes of the retired who have no responsibilities, no claim upon themselves by anyone other than themselves, trapped in themselves. Irresponsibility is ugly whether it occurs at seventeen or seventy. Marriage becomes a contract between two friendly strangers who band together only to satisfy individual needs.

So the story of Ruth and Naomi, two women, strangers bound together in the face of a hostile world, strikes us as strange. The story says that family, parents, children are an invitation to expose ourselves to strangers, to become vulnerable to another, to link our future to some project greater than ourselves. To be in any family, any marriage, is to venture forth like Ruth and Naomi, without guarantees for the future, with only the confidence that the future, even the worst of futures, is more bearable when we bear it with another.

I don't have time to go into the rest of the story, but I can say that, after Ruth and Naomi got to Bethlehem, Naomi got busy and found Ruth a husband. He wasn't much of a husband, but he did the job.

"He's too old for me," said Ruth.

"Old men are good in marriage," said Naomi. "Besides, he's the only man we've got." (This Naomi had been around the block a few times.)

And Ruth bore a son in Bethlehem. Ruth, a woman alone, vulnerable, at a dead end, with no future, no hope, had a child up in Bethlehem. And the child of Ruth was named Obed, and Obed was the father of Jesse, and Jesse was the father of David, and David was eventually the father of Joseph the carpenter, and Joseph was the father of another baby boy born up at Bethlehem named Jesus, Joshua, which means, "God will save."

See? Ruth, a foreign, Moabite woman, through the twistings and turnings of providence, becomes the means of salvation for Israel, for us. Bethlehem's baby reminds us that this is a family story, but it's not just an isolated story about an ordinary family like yours or mine. It's a story about the whole human family, about the way in which God can use your little, ordinary human family from New Jersey in spectacularly wonderful ways. God saves through ordinary people like Ruth, Naomi, Joseph, Mary, and Jesus doing ordinary duties like having babies and putting up with daughters-in-law in ordinary families like yours and mine. If we'll just stick together, through thick and thin, and trust God to use

| our ordinary fidelity to one another to bless the world in
God's extraordinary love.

EXEGETICAL NOTES ON RUTH 1:1–19A

Today's preacher has somewhat of a problem with today's
first lesson. The book of Ruth is far too rich a feast to limit
ourselves to Ruth 1:1–19a. Therefore, early on we make a
decision to preach from the entire novella, letting the assigned lectionary text serve as an introduction to a sermon
on a major portion of Ruth. The beginning of any sermon on
Ruth should be a reading of the entire book at one sitting.
Ruth is set in the time of the Judges, a time when, according
to the last verse in that turbulent book, "Every man did what
was right in his own eyes." Famine is the horrible background for the work. We are in Moab, scene of the earlier
encounters between Abraham and Lot. Moab is where the
two sons of Elimelech of Bethlehem marry Moabite women.
We are out on the fringes, out among a people who are different from the primal family. When these two men die
there are two unattached, unprotected, extremely vulnerable Moabite women, Orpah and Ruth, who must now make
their way among strangers in a difficult world.

The old mother-in-law, Naomi, urges the two Moabite
women to return to their own people. But they stay with
Naomi (the Word says that they "clung" to her, the same
word used in Genesis to describe what happens to a man
and a woman in marriage). I have chosen to preach this
story as a story about God's providence in the middle of our
human family struggles. I think this is fair, considering the
author's development of the personalities and their struggles in Ruth. Also, I encounter this text from Ruth within a
particular pastoral context. By a happy coincidence, it is
Parents' Weekend here in the university, so a theme of God
working in and by our families suggested itself to me. How-

ever, other themes for this material from Ruth could be God's love for outsiders, the peculiar way in which God reaches out to outsiders through faithfulness among God's people. The birth of a son to Ruth and Boaz at the end of the story (4:13) has always been viewed by the church as a kind of foreshadowing of another unexpected birth of a son, Jesus. The son of Ruth and Boaz is in fact an ancestor of King David, who was an ancestor of King Jesus.

Three widows stand before us in a precarious, dangerous predicament. Their husbands are dead, they are among strange people. What will become of them? Although they are foreigners, "outsiders," through their fidelity to Naomi, Ruth and Orpah will find redemption and a surprisingly, unexpectedly open future. Is God active in such ordinary, mundane, and desperate circumstances? That is one of the questions the writer undoubtedly wants us to ask as we encounter this story of Ruth.

Dear Will:

I really didn't like "Ordinary People." I realize that the intent of the sermon was to help us locate our lives in terms of the struggle of Naomi and Ruth to maintain family, but I think the whole strategy of the sermon was a mistake. By concentrating on family, you miss the background story that makes Ruth make sense—namely, why it is so important in Israel for there to be marriage and children. You didn't provide that background for those hearing the sermon, and as a result I think you missed a golden opportunity to help people see that for Christians and Jews the family is not an end in itself, but rather is an institution in service to a larger community.

The move you made in the middle of the sermon, concerning how the current emphasis on the individual undercuts our very understanding of family, was quite good. One of the metaphors that I use about that is that we simply discover that we are "stuck with" certain people for no apparent reason. Family becomes our last reminder that we do not live in a voluntaristic world, since we do not choose our family. We simply wake up one day and discover we have this mother and this father and these brothers and sisters and there's not a damn thing we can do about it.

Your suggestion of how the university becomes part of that strategy was right—namely, that the university is where we try to help people transcend the limits of family. Ironically that is not just a project for making people individuals, but part of the egalitarianism of our society, to make us all equal by making us all free from our histories. That is the reason why the family continues to stand as the great insult to egalitarian policies.

I liked also the moves you made in terms of freedom being identified with the fewest number of attachments. That struck me as peculiarly happy words to say on Parents' Weekend at the university, when people are struggling in that awkward context to reconstitute their familial relationships under new conditions. However, I'm not at all sure that you ought to be trying to address Parents' Weekend at the university in that way. After all, just as the university decides to detach children from their parents, so the church also is about detaching children from their parents. It is not a question of detachment or not, but on what grounds we are detached from one another.

The Parents' Weekend context certainly would encourage you to take up the theme of family, but when you do that you become a chapel in service to the university rather than a chapel in service to the church. I don't mean that those are stark alternatives, and that you cannot be in service to both, but I think how you do it needs more thought than you gave this particular sermon. By trying to address

Parents' Weekend, you lost a story of Israel without which the story of Ruth is unintelligible. The crucial question is not just Ruth's loyalty to Naomi, but Ruth's willingness to become part of Israel and to worship Naomi's God. I thought it quite telling that you didn't pick up that aspect of the text at all, where she said not only would she be part of Naomi's people but she would also worship the God of Naomi's people. Without that God we have no hedge against our children's being abandoned to their peers—a point that was wonderfully made, by the way.

Perhaps another way to put it is that I think you could have done a good deal more with the notion of stranger. Ruth as Moabite was a stranger to the people of Israel, yet Israel, through necessity, was forced to make Moabites part of Israel. Thus Israel proleptically becomes the church, as through Christ we are now, Gentile strangers engrafted into that people. If you had picked up those themes you might have been able to show how family and marriage always involve the joining of strangers in a way that enriches what the Christian community is about. As it was, you simply underwrote the notion that God will use ordinary people in and of themselves, separate from how their ordinariness is a constituent of a wider community.

There is a theme here that I want to mention because it's one I've reflected a lot about, but it's not a criticism of your sermon. I've thought a lot about how liberalism and its goal of detaching people from their near and distant relatives in some ways is a kind of perverse image of the church. Because, as I suggested earlier, the church also is about detachment. So in an odd way what we currently see happening in our society in terms of people being alienated from one another, and in particular from their families, is what the church should also be doing, only on a quite different ground—namely, on the ground of love of God and the community that God has made possible.

That issue is not entirely unrelated to what I think was the main problem with the sermon. It was a deep mistake to ignore the Gospel text in relationship to the text from Ruth. Render unto the emperor the things that are the emperor's and unto God the things that are God's is not unlike the choice that Ruth had to make. By deciding to go with Naomi she had to make clear who the God was that was to make her life intelligible. Her later tricking of Boaz and subsequent marriage are intelligible only within the framework of what community we are to be part of in order to be loyal to God. In the absence of such loyalty the family becomes a destructive institution, too much an entity in itself. I think that you could have dwelt on those conflicts of loyalty in a way that would be quite illuminating, particularly on Parents' Weekend in the university. If we have a god in our society, it's probably more the family than it is the state. You might have worked on render to the family the things that are family's and to God the things that are God's. That would have been upsetting to a good number of families there since, as we know, families finally, like the emperor, want everything. Of course, parents often want everything in the name of securing the freedom of their children. That is the source of so many of the double messages our children receive today. We say, Be free, but by being free that means they are to end up just like us. What we need to tell our children is that they have a destiny that is more determinative than their loyalty to family.

If I were to suggest anything to you, you should start with a different title for the sermon. I think you ought to call it "Extraordinary People" and focus on the place of Israel. Of course Israel is constituted by ordinary people, but what makes those ordinary people so extraordinary is they have been separated out by God to be a sign of God's holiness. So we do not praise ordinary people in and of themselves but insofar as their ordinariness is teleologically oriented to service in God's kingdom.

Two final points: I think it was a mistake not to at least say something about this text as primarily about women. I thought you nicely showed how Ruth's faithfulness ultimately is tied to Jesus' birth (you might have noted that she is mentioned in Matthew's genealogy), but I don't think you emphasized enough that women play a central role in this text. It may well be that women often turn out to be more powerful than men, who think they have the power. It is often pointed out to me when I say that just war is the determinative tradition of the church, even though I'm a pacifist, that that may be a misreading if you remember that women have constituted most of the church and they have not been permitted to go to war. So men have managed to keep women more faithful than we have been through our suppression of their ability to go to war.

Secondly, I think you didn't do enough with the presumption that the first enemy of the family is the church. After all, it is the church that says you do not have to marry since you no longer have to have biological children for the church to be the church. You have an opportunity to show something of the differences between the church and Israel and why we are at once so similar and so different. I realize that these are not issues that seem existentially engaging to people at Parents' Weekend, but at least it would give them a different perspective. As it is, I fear that through this sermon you underwrote the presuppositions so dominant about the family today, and as a result failed to challenge the family in the name of the gospel.

Peace,

Stanley

CHAPTER FIVE

Who Are
These?

All Saints' Sunday
Revelation 7:9–17

*"Who are these, clothed in white robes, and
whence have they come? . . . These are they
who have come out of the great tribulation;
they have washed their robes and made them
white in the blood of the Lamb."*

In *Habits of the Heart,* the sociological study of
Americans in the eighties, there is an interview with a
young adult named "Sheila." When asked about religion, Sheila says, "I consider myself religious, but I
don't know when I've been to church. My religion is
just my own little voice. I guess you could call my religion 'Sheilaism.' " A religious journal designated Sheila
as "The Theologian of the Eighties." Sheila is us.

A Duke student noted recently that, on this campus as
on nearly any other, it is as if religion is the one unmen-
tionable activity. We talk about everything—sex, politics, economics. But religion? "That's *personal,*" we
say. Private. As Sheila says, "Just my own little voice."

In our relativistic age, disagreements over religion
are usually resolved by recourse to, "Well, if it makes
you happy to believe that, that's fine. I believe this. You
believe that. The important thing is what seems right to

69

you, right?'' Religion is my personal opinion—*at the moment.*

And one of the most uncomfortable aspects of religion, for people like us, is that it is old. Who else but religious people would build a building in the 1930s (like this Chapel) that looks a thousand years older than it really is? And we read from an old book with old words. And clergy wear strange, old clothes. My stole was once the equivalent of a Roman necktie. When Western males stopped wearing them around the fifth century, the clergy didn't.

Little wonder that there are folk who say that, if the church really wants to speak to modern people, it had better get its act together and modernize itself. The poor old church had better get with it.

But there is something to be said in our time for not getting with it. There is a peculiar relevance of the irrelevant. Tradition, the past, gives today's Christians not only roots, order, wisdom, stability, conservation, but also *options.* Tradition, far from limiting our focus to the rear view, has a way of enriching the spectrum of our vision. And many of us are dying for want of options.

For many people, ethics is mainly a matter of narrowing life's focus. "I considered one or two possible responses to this problem and I narrowed them down to the one response that seemed right to me.''

Christian people are those who do "what's right.'' But of course, when we are mainly listening to the voice of our own conscience, or deciding on the basis of our personal experience, "what seems right to me,'' right belief or correct action is greatly simplified. Such simplification, however, runs the risk of making us, in G. K. Chesterton's words, "slaves to the opinions of that arrogant oligarchy of those who just happen to be walking about." Many of us have liberated ourselves from the past only to become slaves to the present, and the present is a demanding master.

The past, experienced in church or out, gives us options. African-American history, feminist history, offer options. He had been born, as most of you, in the "right" kind of family on the right side of town. His father was a wealthy cloth merchant. He had a good education, good looks, good friends, and liked good times, good wine, and a good fight. Francis Bernardone grew more serious as he grew older. He was concerned about the plight of the poor, but not overly concerned. Meeting a leper on the road one day (Did you say a victim of AIDS? No, I said leper), he spurred his horse, flinging back a bit of gold to ease his conscience. Suddenly, from nowhere, a great wave of pity swept over the carefree young man. He turned back, dismounted, took all the money out of his pocket, and thrust it into the man's hands. Overcoming his revulsion at the man's sores, he embraced him.

Of course, we know him as *Saint* Francis of Assisi, the young man who walked out of a good position with his old man in order to go to God. As Chesterton said of him, "Francis ran away to God the way some boys run away to the circus."

Now, one can only guess the possibly disruptive effect of my telling a story like that on the options of Duke undergraduates. One of the most disruptive, unsettling, revolutionary acts of the church is in telling stories of the saints, those men and women throughout history who have said "No" to the paucity of options given them by the status quo and said yes to the riches of God. Remembrance gives options.

A graduate student who has been interviewing women at an abortion counseling service near here said that most of the women getting an abortion regret their decision but cited, as the main reason for their abortion, "I had no other option." That doesn't sound like "freedom of choice," does it? "I had no option."

Lack of imagination is a by-product of social amnesia. An inability to remember the saints produces a failure of nerve among today's believers. No options without memory. Remembrance is a potentially revolutionary act.

Which is one of the things I love about this Chapel. To gather here on a Sunday morning is vividly to be reminded none of this began with us. We are debtors whenever we gather for worship. Maya Angelou says, "You have been paid for." Whether we gather on Homecoming or All Saints, our spiritual forebears stare down at us from their perches above. Deborah, Samson, Gideon, Mary, and all the saints. Every time we gather, we join in a divine-human conversation which began long before any of us was born and will continue long after all of us are dead, a conversation far more diverse and rich than our merely contemporary expressions of it. Is that why you love this place? Or could that be why you are threatened by this place?

"I'm getting by the best I can. Oh, yes, I consider myself religious, but I don't make a big show of it. One must learn to adapt, to adjust one's enthusiasm." And you all adapted, adjusted.

And you put on a coat and tie to please your mama on Sunday and go to church. "Yes, Mom. I'm brushing my teeth when I get up in the morning, and taking precautions when I go on a date on Saturday, and oh, yes, just to be safe, I go to the Chapel on Sunday."

But as you enter the Chapel you smell something. Pigeons? It's not English Leather. What is that odor?

But as you look to your left, just as you enter the door,

and see Savonarola and next to him stands Wycliffe, and you realize what you smell. *It's burning flesh.*

So you loosen your tie and fumble for your safety belt when you get to your seat because, surrounded by the saints, you don't know where you'll be by the end of the service. Because in baptism, *you* are a saint.

And one would think preaching would be better here, what with so many placed so high so they can peer over the preacher's shoulder during the sermon. My sermons are judged not only by whether they are interesting, reasonable, and short, but also by whether or not they can endure the scrutiny of the saints. For the faith I'm paid to preach is not my own, or even yours, but that of the church, a two-thousand-year procession which wrote some of its best stuff in blood.

At the base of this lectern there's a bald-headed saint, probably Ambrose. He has a scroll and a quill in his hands. I once thought he was down there as a symbol of divine inspiration—the saint taking notes from the Lord. Then one day it hit me: He's down there, right under the pulpit, taking notes from me! I'm accountable, not just to Dr. Brodie and the trustees, but to the saints. It's kind of scary for a preacher.

Fred Craddock, who has preached here, tells of returning to a little church of his childhood in Tennessee. He had not been there in years. Walking in the sanctuary, he noted that they had purchased new stained-glass windows since he had been there. Admiring the windows, he saw set at the bottom of each window the name of the donor of the window. But he recognized none of the names.

"You must have had many new folks join this church since I was a boy," said Fred to one of the members. "I don't recognize a single name."

"Oh, those people aren't members here. This town

hasn't grown a bit since you were a child; neither has our church. We bought those windows from a company all the way over in Italy. They were made for a church in St. Louis and, when they arrived, none of them would fit. So the company said they were sorry, they would make new windows, and told the church in St. Louis to sell them wherever they could. We bought the windows from them."

"But don't you want to remove these names?" asked Fred.

"Well, we thought about it. We're just a little church. Not many of us here, never any new people. So we like to sit here on Sunday morning surrounded by the names of people other than ourselves."

Dear Will:

I think the sermon on All Saints was just about perfect. It was not only theologically profound but it seemed to be a beautiful exemplification of the art of the sermon which you always accuse me of missing. For example, I did not miss the way the ending of the sermon really provided an alternative for the beginning. You begin with Sheila, who has no one to help tell her who she is, and you end with that wonderful Craddock story where people are surrounded by the saints.

Moreover, I thought the way you used the building in this sermon was extraordinary. One of the things I admire is the way you are able to leave certain things unsaid as you preach. For example, you could have said that such buildings are in fact our memory. As long as we have been given such gifts as this our memory cannot fail, though we may fail to use it. I feel quite sure that you had thought of that

74

but you left it unsaid and instead used the statues and windows to remind us that the saints are indeed dangerous.

My temptation, of course, would have been to start quoting Metz on what it means for the church to be a community of dangerous memory. Rather than using more conceptual machinery to say what people would not get, you instead gave concreteness to that through the use of the building, and in particular the Francis example. Moreover, you did not get into the business of how everyone in the church is at once a saint, yet we have some whom we hold out for special recognition. You were wise to avoid that, though it is not a matter to be ultimately avoided.

What I would like to say about it is that the church is a community of saints just to the extent it can recognize saints who shine among us. Saints are nothing without a community of memory, willing to let certain people stand within judging us and calling our own lives into question. So to be a communion of saints makes saints possible.

You did not go into the whole business of the critique of saints by Protestants. We have to say that the Protestant Church has been left deficient just to the extent that we do not recognize and/or acknowledge saints. Indeed one of our deep difficulties today is that, unlike the Catholics, we have no means of beatification; instead beatification comes only through the very selective memories. It has much to do with the nature of authority, and that might have been a theme worth developing, since that is at the heart of Sheilaism. In a world with no authority you simply cannot have saints. As a result, you are left to the tyranny of your own choice.

I thought particularly courageous was your use of the abortion example. I know the temptation is just not to mention that issue at all, but I thought you did it extremely well. For you indicated that the problem is not that we lack choice, but that the choices we have are self-imposed necessities due to a failure of imagination. Moreover, what failure of imagination means in that context is really a failure of community, where young women are given alternatives through their friends. I mention that in relationship to the authority question because I think some people might not have seen how the abortion example worked in relationship to the larger theme of sainthood, because the relationship between choice, memory, sainthood, and authority was not necessarily displayed. However, again I can hardly be critical as it seems to me that it's best that you let people make the connections.

Indeed, I think that one of the things I am trying to learn about the art of the sermon is how you do not want to say too much. For if you say too much, then people do not do any work as part of their hearing of the sermon. It is important that you give images that draw on our common store of associations such that people can make connections themselves and thus be drawn into the actual activity of the Word. The problem is what it means to do that in a culture where there is not that large a store of common association and images, or what store there is is deeply degraded. Obviously it will vary from topic to topic, but it seems you found a happy way to do it in this sermon.

Isn't it wonderful when All Saints falls on Homecoming? I thought you did well to stay away from that as the occasion while mentioning it just briefly to really support your main point. The whole business of what it means to live on the basis of others' gifts is a theme that needs more emphasis in our current religious practices.

If I have any criticism of the sermon it would be that you did not put the saints in an appropriately eschatological framework. It was fine for you to assume the text from Revelation, but I think you could have at least suggested that the saints are not just past, somehow back there. They are here among us now as we belong to the communion of saints that God has made possible through the eschatological shape of our existence. In that way you would have brought the whole sermon to a climax, pointing again to the Eucharist, where in celebrating today we believe that we celebrate with those who have gone before and who are to come. I do not think you can overemphasize today the necessary interrelationship between Word and sacrament. The deep difficulty is knowing how to do that in a way that does not appear artificial.

I knew you were bound to get one right. It was a joy to have heard it.

Peace,

Stanley

CHAPTER SIX

One Tough Master?

Twenty-fourth Sunday after Pentecost
Matthew 25:14–28

"Master, I knew that you were a harsh man,
reaping where you did not sow, and gathering
where you did not scatter seed; so I was afraid,
and I . . . hid your talent in the ground" (NRSV).

You know with whom we identify in this story. We are on the side of the little one-talent man. Perhaps because few of us are overburdened with talent, perhaps because we love stories of the little guy who makes good. The woman who stood up to the powers of the IRS and won. The student who went one-on-one with the mighty university and triumphed. We're on the side of the little guy.

Toward the end of his time with us, Jesus told a story. This parable of the talents comes toward the end of his life, just before Jesus was to go away.

A man is going away on a journey. He is rich, for when he calls his servants to him and disburses his money, he gives them a lot of money. To one he gives five talents. A talent is the largest currency known in the ancient Near East. We're talking from sixty to seventy-five pounds of pure silver, a great fortune. To another he gives two talents, over a hundred pounds of silver, and to the third servant one talent, about fifteen years of wages in one lump sum.

Then the master leaves town, which probably increases our sympathy for the little one-talent servant. The master is not only rich, he is an absentee landlord, probably living up somewhere in the Northeast while his servants slave for him in the mines of Appalachia or the textile mills of North Carolina. Just when they could use his advice on investments, he dumps this ridiculously huge amount of money on his once-poor servants and departs on a cruise.

Servants one and two wheel and deal with their master's money. Servant number three does the cautious thing, the right thing. He has only one talent, not five or two; still, as we said, one talent is a lot of money. So he digs a hole, buries it, stands guard over it, keeps it safe and sound.

He doesn't go out and risk his master's money like servants one and two. He buries it. Burying was the only way for most people to protect what they had in that day. The rabbis ruled that if you entrusted some money to a person and the money was lost, if that person had prudently hidden the money in the ground, then he was not liable for the loss. Rabbi Samuel said, "Money can only be guarded [by placing it] in the earth." By burying the money, the third servant is assured of a favorable judgment when his master returns. He has acted responsibly, prudently, wisely. The same way that you or I would have acted.

What is more, the third servant must have had a course in business ethics. (It's a short course.) He, of all the servants, appears to be the only one who considers the ethics of his stewardship. It is his master's money, after all, not his. He has no right to blow his master's money in wild speculation. What is more, usury, the obtaining of interest, was still frowned on in Israel. He does the right thing. He buries the money.

Eventually, the master returns and wants to know how things have gone in his absence. Servants one and two report that things have gone well for them. They took the master's money, invested it, and got great results. The master is thrilled, so thrilled that he lets them keep all the money. "Enter into the joy of your master," he tells them.

Servant number three also has great results. "Here, master, you gave me one talent. Here is your one talent back. All safe and sound. I didn't waste any of it. Didn't risk any of it. Didn't blow it on any crackpot business schemes or loan it to any of my cronies. I knew that you were a hard man, the type of master who likes to squeeze blood out a turnip, who expects to reap where he didn't sow, to gather where he did not scatter. Here all safe and sound is your talent."

And the master says, "You wicked, slothful servant. Blood out of a turnip, my eye. If that were so, if I were all that hardhearted, then one would have at least expected you to put this talent in insured CD's at an FDIC-backed bank! Then I would have at least gotten a measly 6 percent. Take what he has and give it to the one who has ten talents."

We do not like this story. The little guy just got clobbered for doing what was right, for doing what was prudent, for doing what we would have done. We do not like this story.

The rich get richer. The poor get shafted. By the way, Jesus told much more likable stories. They were passing the collection plate in church one Sunday and people were placing large bills in the plate, checks, American Express cards, and there was this one little poor widow who put in all she had, just one little quarter. Jesus praised that poor widow, but not the rich.

We like those stories where the little guy goes to the head of the class and the big guy gets clobbered.

We don't like this story with the trembling little man, clutching his one little talent, shaking, saying, "Master, I knew you were tough, reaping where you don't sow. So I was careful, prudent, cautious. Those are great Christian virtues, aren't they?"

"You wicked little wretch! Take what he has—give it to the others."

By the way, if I should ever be dumb enough to give you a hundred dollars of my money, I definitely *do not* want you to go invest it. I want you to bury it. I'd rather have the principal with no interest than to risk having no principal.

And what do you think of this master? That is the question left in our minds by the end of the story. Who is this master? We know only that he is rich, that he went away and then finally came back, that he risked a fabulous amount of money on three servants and then gave all the money back to two of the servants while taking it all away from the third.

Our first inclination is to agree with the third servant's assessment of the master. "Master, I knew that you were a hard man, reaping where you do not sow, gathering where you haven't even scattered. You are a hard man. Tough." But come to think of it, that's only the third servant's opinion of the master. The master doesn't confirm or deny this opinion of his business methods. Which leaves the matter open for us to decide. What do you think of this master?

When the story begins, we are not inclined to think of the master as a hardhearted business man. In fact, we might think just the opposite. How many hardhearted business people do you know who will drop fifteen years of wages on one of their employees and then leave town?

As the story opens, you might say that this master is anything but hardhearted. He appears to be softheaded, lavishing about a thousand pounds of sterling silver on three servants, placing no restrictions on what to do with it, and then leaving town.

And when he comes back for the accounting, for the judgment, that's when we expect the gavel to come down, that's when this allegedly hardhearted man will let his servants have it. Which is exactly what he does for servants one and two. He lets them have it. All of it. He asks them to account for what they've done with the money and, when he finds out that they have done a lot with the money, he turns around and gives them all of the money. "Enter into the joy of your master."

Does that sound hardhearted to you?

No, it is only when the third servant, our man, the little guy, stands up to render account, that we are told (by him), "Master, I knew you were a hardhearted man. Tough. Reaping where you haven't even sown. Here is your talent, Mr. Tough Guy. All safe and sound. Tell me what a good little boy I've been."

Did he say reaping where he did not sow? What did they think the master was doing when he threw that thousand pounds of silver at them? He was sowing! Is he unjustified in expecting some harvest for that sort of sowing?

What do you think of this master?

The dean was about to go away on sabbatical. So he called in the department chairs together. To one the dean gave five departments, to another two departments, and to another one. Then the dean went to study flora in Honolulu. The one who had received five de-

partments got busy and established five more departments. So, also, the one who received two departments
established two more. But the one who received one
department sat in his office and attempted to maintain
the status quo.

After a long time the dean returned (in a Hawaiian
shirt), and called in all three before the Academic
Council. The chair who had received the five departments presented those and five new ones. "Well done,
good chair," said the dean. "I make you an assistant
dean. Enter into the joy of Allen Building." He said the
same to the one who had made two new departments.

The one who had received only one department
said, "Dean, I knew that you were a hard dean, so I
was afraid. I didn't take any chances, didn't hire anybody, made no new courses, didn't join the NAS [Na-
tional Association of Scholars] or the SPCA—just kept
office hours and filled out reports."

"You wicked and slothful department chair!" said the
dean. "You heard what I did when I was at Stanford,
how I took names and knocked heads! You ought to
have added to the faculty load, set up new courses,
taken out ads in the *Chronicle,* and found new majors
so that when I returned *Newsweek* would rate us higher
than Princeton! Hard dean, my eye. This is Duke. You've
got tenure, for heaven's sake. What could I do to you if I
wanted to? Lord, deliver me from these academic bean
counters and give me some people who want to wheel
and deal! Take the department and give it to someone
who knows how to deal—put this little college on the
map!"

"I knew you to be a hard man." Really, now, does he
know the master? Who is the master? Is he a hardhearted, tough miser of a master who expects to reap
where he hasn't even sown? (Thanks to William A.

Beardslee, "A Conversation About the Parable of the Talents," *Pulpit Digest,* Oct. 1985, pp. 44–45, for this story.)

Or is he an extravagant, reckless wheeler-dealer, whose faith in his servants is exceeded only by his generosity? He gave them all that he had. Every cent. Is it hardhearted of him to expect them to be as reckless as he? And when they come back to render account, you'd think that, if he is pleased, he might let them keep some of the interest they have earned. No, he tells them to keep it all, interest and principal.

Who is this master?

Jesus had some funny ideas about business. (A sower went out to sow and he carefully plowed each furrow and then carefully, ever so carefully, put seed spaced exactly six inches apart in a straight line . . .)

No, Jesus said, a sower went out to sow and just threw seed everywhere. Slinging seed. Of course some fell on rocky ground, some among the weeds, some on good ground—and you get an uneven harvest with this sort of sowing.

Master, we knew you to be the sort of man who expected to harvest in much the same way as you sow, recklessly.

He said, "Naw, just let 'em grow together. We'll sort it all out later."

Who is this master?

And moving from sloppy farming to outrageous shepherding, Jesus said, "The good shepherd lays down his life for the sheep." What? You show me a shepherd who will lay down his life for a $9.95 plus postage sheep and I'll show you a dumb shepherd. Or else an unbelievably extravagant shepherd.

Who is this master? And what would your life be as his servant?

Dear Will:

I found your sermon "One Tough Master?" to be just a bit too obscure. This is where I'm going to tell you what kind of sermon you should have preached. I admire the way that you were trying to set the passage up for the congregation in a manner that made them consider the very nature of God. But I'm not sure you did it in a strong enough fashion, because the narratives they are going to read into your sermon are not the narratives you hope will be read.

One of my favorite quotations is from Cardinal Souhard, who says, "To be a witness does not consist in engaging in propaganda nor even in stirring people up, but in being a living mystery. It means to live in a way that one's life would not make sense if God did not exist." I take it that's what you were trying to do in this sermon—namely, you were trying to ask the audience to enter imaginatively into this parable so that they would ask, "What kind of God would make sense of coming down on this poor servant who thought he should ensure that the money would be returned in full?"

I approve of the strategy, but I don't think you gave the congregation enough to make the strategy successful. Indeed, I'm a bit embarrassed by calling it a strategy, since that makes it sound manipulative. I don't think you were trying to be manipulative, but rather to elicit in your congregation the same kind of position that Jesus' hearers were in. But I don't think that happened, because too much remained having to do with the issue of the talents themselves. I think it was a mistake, for example, for you to suggest how much a talent was worth in the ancient world. I think that kind of historical point doesn't help us understand the parable.

What is missing in your sermon is the whole eschatological frame that makes the parable make sense. You are right to call attention to what kind of master would ask this, but it is not just the master, but rather the master's mission that makes it make sense—namely, that now in the presence of this man Jesus the universe is facing its destiny. So confronted, we can no longer play if safe, but must live in a way that risk is unavoidable.

In that sense this passage has been used to underwrite capitalist presuppositions about entrepreneurship. It's ironical that the last thing in the world modern capitalists want to do is take a risk, since modern corporations depend not on risk-taking, but on the domestication of risk. What a modern businessman cannot stand is unpredictability. Knowing exactly what you want the market to do, and what is required if you are to be a big business, means knowing what the next five, and if possible ten, years are going to be like.

I'm sure you thought of how the passage had been used to underwrite certain kinds of economic ideologies in the past. You wanted to avoid that, and so didn't raise it at all. However, I think you needed to raise it and to suggest how the kingdom of God really is about risk. Jesus' preaching of the kingdom puts us in a position where we have to live unsure of the outcome. So living creates necessities that force us to be a people that we otherwise could not be.

I often think about this in relationship to my being a pacifist. People like to confront pacifists with "What would you do if . . . ?" and you then get detailed accounts of situations where it would seem necessary for you to use violence. However, what it means to be nonviolent is to create necessities that force us imaginatively into alternatives that would otherwise not have been present. For example, if you think of that little story in *Watership Down,* the one I used in *A Community of Character,* where Hazel, soon after the rabbits escape from their original warren, is confronted with having to cross a river with them. It looks as if they are going to have to swim across the river, and one of the smaller rabbits who has come with them is not strong enough to do it. The militaristic one among them says, "We'll just have to leave him behind," and that makes all the sense in the world, as otherwise they will all be destroyed by the dogs that are chasing them. Hazel, however, who really isn't the leader yet, says, "You're right. You go ahead. But I'm going to stay here with the weaker rabbit since I got him into this." That forces one of the other rabbits, who is the intellectual among the bunch, to say, "I wonder if we could put a rabbit on this board and float him across?" Moral and theological commitment creates imaginative responses to necessity.

I think that is what Jesus was about in this parable of the kingdom. He was suggesting that the kingdom forces us through its gifts into new configurations which create a world that otherwise would not be. I always think about this parable in relationship to Paul's understanding of the gifts. The church is built up out of the many different gifts of its members, which have new configurations in the light of being a community of the kingdom. It doesn't make the risk go away; rather, it creates risk that enhances our gifts.

I also read this parable against the issues raised by Martha Nussbaum in *The Fragility of Goodness*. As you know, Nussbaum argues that the virtues themselves make our life more fragile, that is, more susceptible to luck. My way of putting it is that the world of the courageous is different from the world of the coward. The courageous live in a more dangerous world than the coward, exactly because they are courageous. So if you are to be courageous, you may well have to expose your life to dangers that the coward doesn't even know exist.

Nussbaum is right in assuming that this kind of interrelationship exists between the virtues and luck. Only we Christians don't call it luck, we call it grace. I do not believe our world is constituted by something called dumb luck, but rather that we live in a world of providential care through which God has called us as members of God's church to exemplify the richness and diversity of God's kingdom. It does involve risk, but those risks turn out to be grace.

Obviously all of this makes sense only if God is the kind of God we find in Jesus of Nazareth. What you make a mistake doing is isolating these parables from their eschatological context. I would have urged you to have situated who the master is in a much more determinative Christological fashion. I think what I'm asking you to do is to not indulge examples like the dean leaving and putting people in charge of more or fewer departments. (By the way, that's a bad analogy anyway, as good department chairmen do not become chairmen of more departments, but would have increased their faculty.) Rather, take more time in your sermon to hammer on the significance of who this Jesus was and trust your people to hear that life in a way that makes sense of their own lives.

I'm a bit embarrassed by this response as I've tried to avoid telling you what you should have preached on rather than what you did preach on. There are many things that every passage invites, as the scripture is inexhaustible in its resources because our God is inexhaustible. However, for some reason I just could not understand this sermon in terms of its rationale vis-à-vis the text, so I had to tell you what I thought you should have preached about.

Peace,

Stanley

CHAPTER SEVEN

The Day of the Lord

Twenty-third Sunday after Pentecost
Amos 5:18–24

"Woe to you who desire the day of the Lord! . . .
'I hate, I despise your feasts,
and I take no delight in your solemn assemblies.' "

This is Sunday, the Lord's Day. This is the day when we worship. That's what I first taught at Duke Divinity School, worship. I am sort of an expert on worship. Proper behavior on Sunday, the Lord's Day.

Which means that I have some definite opinions about how worship ought to be. I have an image about how worship is when it is done right, and I expect that you have an image, too, of how worship ought to be. That's why many of you are here on this Lord's Day, because, in your opinion, Duke Chapel does it right. Here is your idea of "good" worship.

I have my own pet peeves and prejudices about "good" worship. For instance, I'm not much on chatter before the service. We put a note in the bulletin, at the top of the first page, telling you not to chatter during the prelude, but sometimes you still do. I don't like that. Another thing—I don't like preachers with "stained glass" voices. Know what I'm talking about? "A blessed welcome to you this blessed morning. Now, let us all rise and turn to hymn 435." I don't like that. Children's sermons? I don't like them. If the preacher wants to star on "Uncle Bill's Funhouse," let him do it at a time other than Sunday. "May we pray?" I don't like that either. What if some Sunday somebody shouted, "No, you may not"? It's "Let us pray."

Plastic flowers (tacky), all male ushers, good-looking preachers—I don't like them. And I'm sure that, if you were doing the talking, you would have your list. (Preachers with Southern accents, cute remarks from the pulpit, homiletical attacks on the dean of students . . .) You don't like it.

Yet how often have we asked, What does *God* like about worship? What does God expect from a Sunday morning? Back to my liturgical thoughts: A primary purpose of our Sunday praise and prayer is *location*. We don't just worship anywhere. We come to a place, a location, a special location. On Sunday morning we get our bearings, so to speak, locating ourselves within a sometimes chaotic and confusing cosmos. Perhaps that is why we build our places of worship bigger, costlier than they need be. It takes four football players to move the Duke Chapel altar.

It became the custom in the church to build our buildings always oriented the same way, facing east. Even when, as with our Chapel, we're facing sort of north, we still call it "east."

Worship locates us. When you're a student, far from home, this chapel can be a place where you are able once again to be embraced by the familiar and the predictable. Everything may be cut loose in our lives, but when we come in on Sunday, things are again tied down, just where we left them at home, comfortable, reassuring, linked to the past.

Sunday is therefore the day to affirm ("I believe in God the Father Almighty, Maker of heaven and earth . . . "), to confirm ("This is my Father's world: I rest me in the thought . . . "), to order in grand procession the eternal verities.

In church, furniture tends to be heavy, bolted down, fixed, immovable. We have a rule in the Chapel. If you get married here, you have to take it, in the words of our wedding guidelines, "as is." No moving, rearranging, or dislocation permitted here.

And yet sometimes, as we are busy affirming, confirming, ordering, locating, there is a dislocating intrusion. When Sunday regularity hardens into stifling stability, and Sunday is a day only for reiteration of royally approved definitions of reality, and worship is but the embodiment of the establishment, sometimes there is dislocating intrusion.

Such, I think, is today's word from the prophet Amos. We have begun, as we usually do, with ourselves, asking what we want from worship. Now what does God want? What is God's definition of "good" worship?

"Woe to you who desire the day of the Lord!" Why do you want to get close to God, to celebrate a day with the Lord? "It is darkness, and not light." To come to God is to flee from a lion only to be embraced by a grizzly. Or to arrive breathless into the safety of your own house, there to be bitten by a rattler. Here is darkness, not light.

Amos is talking about the Day of the Lord. That hoped-for, prayed-for day when God would at last come down and be with God's people, that day when the presence of God would no longer be something high, far off, and distant, but here.

"Maranatha!" ("Come, Lord Jesus") is probably the earliest of Christian prayers. Come, Day of the Lord. Come, be with us.

"You want that day?" says Amos. Be careful! That day is gloom, not light, a bear, a poison snake.

And then Amos hears God speak some of the most terrifying, dislocating words in the Bible. "I hate, I despise your feasts, and I take no delight in your solemn assemblies." Bring your offerings up to the altar? "I will not accept them, . . . I will not look upon [them]. Take away from me the racket of your songs; to the melody of your pipe organs I will not listen."

God says, Your worship makes me sick. The smell of your offerings, your sweet incense rising into the rafters, nauseates me. Your lovely four-part harmony hurts my ears. Take it away!

Go ahead, says God, sing your little songs—I don't like your kind of music. Preach your sermons, pray your prayers—my ears are closed.

What does God want? What is "good" worship? How are we supposed to celebrate properly the "Lord's Day"?

You know the words: "Let justice roll down like waters, and righteousness like an ever-flowing stream."

There may be gods, there may be religions, for whom worship is but the beating of a drum, the ringing of a bell, the burning of sweet incense, or repetition of high-sounding words. Israel's religion, Israel's God, is not one of them.

You know what I love on Sunday morning? A joyous chorus from Handel; a clear trumpet, sounded from our organ, by Purcell; to see that silver cross lifted and moving in stately procession down that aisle; coat-and-tied, chaste sophomores attentively seated on the second row. That's what I like.

"You know what I love on a Lord's Day?" says the Lord. "Justice rolling down like Niagara, righteousness flowing like the Mississippi, that's what I like," says the Lord.

In the exodus, Moses is sent to Pharaoh to ask for a few days off for the Hebrew slaves so "We can go out in the desert and worship our God."

"You can worship your God right here in Egypt," replies Pharaoh.

Moses continues to plead, "Let us go so we can worship our God." Pharaoh continues to refuse. Ten plagues and much pain later, Pharaoh consents. "OK, Hebrews, get out of here and don't look back until you are someplace other than Egypt."

At last they are free to worship. Well, they get out in the desert, free, ready to worship God. But how? Nobody has ever worshiped this God before, at least not for a long time. They've forgotten how. Are there directions? Anybody got a copy of the hymnal?

Then God takes Moses up on the mountain, while the people await further rubrics. "I am the Lord your God, who brought you out of the land of Egypt," says God in a voice like Charlton Heston, "so that you might worship me."

"Yes, yes," Moses replies, "but how are we supposed to do that? Do you like gospel music or are you more into Gregorian chant? Do you like the King James Version or the *revised* Revised Standard Version?"

"You know what I like?" says the Lord. "I like the kind of worship where you shall have no other gods before me. You do not kill. You don't steal. You don't commit adultery. That's my idea of a good time on Sunday. The ethical linked to the liturgical." Moses found it is a disrupting experience to worship this God!

95

What we want is Sunday as a time of stability. Our ministers become managers of conventional definitions of reality; our liturgies, an embodiment of the establishment. There is the King on the throne, here are we, all in a line of bolted-down pews. Sunday is about the eternal continuity of the known, old world.

Yet here comes a disruptive, prophetic word, a linguistic assault upon the presumed, fixed, royal world. Amos's contemporaries longed for a "day of the Lord," assuming that day would be in continuity with present arrangements, assuming that present arrangements are God's arrangements, that current social, political, economic configurations are divinely ordained.

No, says Amos, in words that shatter the presently legitimated order. No. On the Lord's Day, the world ends. The granite walls of the post office, city hall, and even your chapels melt under the blast of God's breath. That's your Day of the Lord. The established, royal world cannot tolerate prophetic speech about the end of the world. Liberal academic religion, so comfortable and adjusted to present arrangements, only mildly uneasy with the status quo, purges apocalyptic talk of the end from Sunday morning. For if a prophet named Amos or Jesus ever stood up and announced the end, that would shatter the present order. The end of an old world has power to evoke a new world; termination leads to evocation.

"I hate, I despise your feasts, . . . the noise of your songs. . . . Let justice roll down like waters, and righteousness like an ever-flowing stream." How are we doing, Lord?

An evening with the Durham Bulls is more racially, culturally integrated than a Sunday morning in Duke Chapel.

What we have here is a prophetic, linguistic assault on the establishment, poetic delegitimation of present configurations of power. But we don't want prophets. We want ministers who are managers of consensus, temple functionaries who scurry around the altar on Sundays in a desperate attempt to keep our known world intact, reassuring us of the eternal stability of the status quo, "God's in his heaven:/All's right with the world."

The known, fixed, royal world is disrupted by prophetic, poetic speech about the end of that world.

A couple of years ago, I was the host for Will Campbell, ascerbic but brilliant Baptist novelist and prophet. It was Sunday; we were walking up the walkway, through the woods, toward the Chapel, my favorite way to approach the Chapel on a Sunday. Bells were ringing, early Sunday sun glistened off the Chapel tower. It was glorious, beautiful. I was proud, and felt that this visitor was probably impressed. He's from Nashville.

Then, as the trees cleared and the Chapel rose before us in all its stately grandeur, I heard Campbell mutter, "Humph! He's come a long way from Bethlehem."

Dear Will:

I have to admit the way you began this sermon hit my prejudices to a tee. I have a room full of views about worship. So your beginning meant I was instantly inscribed into that narrative. It was wonderfully humorous, and at the same time did some teaching about what worship might and should be like. I thought also you set it up nicely to hear the radicalness of Amos's words. The way you suggested that the very size of our churches and their

97

beauty is meant to reassure us that we are safe from the Day of the Lord I thought was extremely effective.

I think the only note that might have sounded a bit stronger would be to challenge the very assumption that worship is dependent on our moral formation, but that worship *is,* rather, our moral formation. The phrase you used is "the ethical linked to the liturgical," but I think what you want to say is the liturgical is the moral and the moral is the liturgical when we understand what this God requires of us.

What you missed is the whole sacrificial context in Amos. The picture we have is something like this, I think: The people had come to think in Amos's day that God was basically appeased by sacrificial offerings. They could then do anything they wanted to with the rest of their moral life as long as they did the appropriate sacrifices. Thus the form of the community as displayed by the Decalogue had become secondary to the life of worship understood as sacrifice. Amos, in condemning worship, made the moral life more significant than the life of sacrifice.

The problem with that picture is that there is no indication in Amos that sacrifice is abrogated. Indeed when we Christians read it that way, we lose any possibility of understanding Jesus and/or our own lives. For Amos is not condemning the necessity of sacrifice. He is asking what sacrifice is about, given the kind of God who has called Israel. In Christ, sacrifice is called for exactly because God is willing to sacrifice God's own life so that the world might know there is an alternative to the world's mode of sacrifice. Therefore, for us ethics and sacrifice cannot be separated but are in fact one.

We cannot lose this, particularly as a eucharistic people. For us Protestants, the language of sacrifice is repressed because we think of sacrifice as making oblations to an angry God. Since we don't want our God to be angry, we don't think we ought to be making sacrifices. What we forget in so trivializing the notion of sacrifice is that in the eucharistic celebration the great good news is that we have been made part of God's sacrifice so that the world might have life. We now become the worthy lambs that can end all other sacrificial systems.

For example, I think that war is often thought of in a moralistic fashion exactly because we think war is about killing. But what war often offers us is the possibility of sacrificing and, in particular, sacrificing to a cause that is greater than we are. That is the reason that the place of women in relationship to war is oftentimes so misunderstood, as women have traditionally been the ones who supported war, exactly because they have thought it was so important in the past to sacrifice their sons for the higher good.

We believe the sacrifice that we become in the Eucharist is the end to such worldly sacrificial systems. Therefore there can be no separation of the sacrifice in the Eucharist and the moral life of the community. That is why Amos condemns Israel, because the worship has become a way of establishing the status quo, which you so nicely indicate, rather than challenging the status quo.

I loved the way you ended the sermon with Will's off-hand comment about the Chapel being such a long way from Bethlehem. I must admit I like to throw out that kind of one-liner myself, and we surely need them, but I'm not sure Will Campbell and I are responsible when we do so. As you know, I've just come back from Europe, and when you see Notre Dame you are humbled by it. When you see the gospel hewn out in stone and windows you know this was a poor person's church, because in a preliterate culture that is the way you learned the story. So I think it is not unthinkable that a sacrificial people might build Duke chapels, but the problem comes when the building is inhabited by people who are not ready to be sacrificial.

I think these matters are more complex, and I'm not sure how to get to them.

Peace,

Stanley

CHAPTER EIGHT

Now

First Sunday of Advent
Mark 13:32–37

*"It is like a man going on a journey, when he
leaves home and puts his servants in charge,
each with his [or her] work."*

Our parable takes place in Galilee, in a world of absentee landlords and servants who are left on their own for years at a time. "You do not know when the time will come," says Jesus. "It is like a man going on a journey, when he leaves home and puts his servants in charge, each with his work."

Here is a parable about masters and servants, employers and employees, about those who have and those who don't have, and those who don't have who work for those who have.

You know where our sympathies lie. In stories, we are always for the little guy, the have-nots. Our sympathies are not with this absentee landlord, but rather with his servants. Where was the master going on a journey? It was December, the days were getting short and cold. Each day it was a longer walk to the barn to feed the livestock as wind swept across now-frozen winter fields.

"You boys take care of things for the winter," the master had said. "I'm out of here. Write me in Palm Beach and tell me how things are going, when you thaw out."

And you know whose side we are on. The master is the man in Manhattan who owns the mine in West Virginia, the one lounging by the pool in L.A. while he clips coupons from his sweatshops in Hong Kong. It is like a man going on a journey who puts his servants in charge.

There must have been many absentee owners in Galilee, for this is not the only story Jesus told about them. "Who then is the faithful and wiser servant . . . ? Blessed is that servant whom his master when he comes will find [hard at work]. . . . But if that wicked servant says to himself, 'My master is delayed,' and begins to beat his fellow servants, and eats and drinks with the drunken, the master of that servant will come on a day when he does not expect him and at an hour he does not know, and will punish him" (Matt. 24:45–51).

Elsewhere: "For it will be as when a man going on a journey called his servants and entrusted to them his property; to one he gave five talents, to another two, to another one. . . . Then he went away" (Matt. 24:14–15).

Or, "A man planted a vineyard, and set a hedge around it, and dug a pit for the wine press, and built a tower, and let it out to tenants, and went into another country" (Mark 12:1).

Out in Galilee, there was a great deal of coming and going, presence and absence.

Whenever the master is absent, it is an occasion for a test of the servants.

"Now, class, I'm going to go down the hall to the principal's office to get a three-pronged plug so we can see our filmstrip, *Rubber Cultivation in Malaysia.* I'm going down that hall. But I'm leaving the door open. Mrs. Moffat, across the hall, will be listening for me, if there's trouble. I hope that I can trust you, that you will prove to me that I can trust you. Now I'm leaving, and I had better not hear a word out of you."

Absence is a test; the return is occasion for accounting. "Johnny, what were you doing on top of my desk?" Jesus' stories of the master's absence are stories about testing. And a servant who can be trusted only when the master is present is a worthless servant.

Today we begin the season of Advent, a time in which we prepare for the Advent of the Messiah. The Babe at Bethlehem is the presence of God, Emmanuel, God with us.

And we long for that presence. "Come, Thou Long-Expected Jesus," "O Come, O Come, Emmanuel," these are Advent hymns. "Return for the sake of thy servants," pleads Isaiah in today's first lesson. "O that thou wouldst rend the heavens and come down,/that the mountains might quake at thy presence/ . . . that the nations might tremble at thy presence!" (Isa. 63:17; 64:1–2).

The prophet pleads for presence. If God would split the skies and come stand among us, irrefutable presence, how much easier would faithfulness be, so the argument goes. "We have all become like one who is unclean,/ . . . our righteous deeds are like a polluted garment./We all fade like a leaf,/and our iniquities . . . take us away./There is no one that calls upon thy name," laments Isaiah. Why? "For thou hast hid thy face from us."

Absence produces faithlessness. When the master goes on a journey, there is a test, which we often flunk. Come, thou long-expected Jesus.

It is a story, today's parable of the absentee landlord, of absence, of the dry places when there is no one either to stand beside us or to look over our shoulders. It is in these great gaps, these times of absence, that the trouble begins when there is no master, no one taking names, no supervisor walking the assembly line, and Mrs. Moffat runs into the office breathless, warning, "Mrs. Jones, you had better get back to your class!"

The way I figure it, most of the New Testament is concerned with this problem of absence. When Jesus was with us, in the flesh, that was one thing. From his own voice we could hear, "Rise, let us be going," and "Fear not!" There was always the possibility of the healing touch, the reassuring word, the guiding light. But in the meantime, in the absence, in the valley between his first advent and the next, what of us?

Is not this the great issue in the whole last two thirds of John's Gospel? The disciples asking, always asking, "Lord, where are you going? Can we go too? Who is going to stay with us while you're gone?"

Mark is wrestling with the same problem in the passage, "It is like a man going on a journey, when he leaves home and puts his servants in charge. . . ."

We pray for the advent, for the presence of Jesus among us. In the Eucharist, Holy Communion, we proclaim the "real presence" of Christ in bread and wine, in our sharing of food and drink. Today's parable suggests that we speak so much of presence because we have so much absence. We've never known any time with Jesus except time of absence, between the time after his first advent and time before the next. Absence. We pray, we read, we listen, we eat and drink, and still something rises in the heart to meet the prophetic words, "Thou hast hid thy face from us."

In this service, here in the Chapel, you may feel

God's near presence, may feel that, if the heavens are not rent asunder, they are at least somewhat ajar so that a smidgen of light peers through and you are reassured.

But you will shortly leave this place, go back to the office, back to exams, back to the dorm, or the kitchen sink, and prayer may not come as easily as here. The presence will not be as sure as in this blessed bread and wine. Hunger for God, temporarily assuaged in Chapel, will rise again, and your Monday prayer will be, "Thou hast hid thy face from us."

Jesus warned us. "It [will be] like a man going on a journey, when he leaves home and puts his servants in charge, each with his work."

Did you hear that? In the initial shock of the absence ("going on a journey, when he leaves home"), did you hear the "puts his servants in charge, each with his [or her] work"?

The story is a parable of absence, of masters who leave, go away. And in listening to the story, we're apt to hear that and nothing else. Absence. But the story is also a message about the meantime. How then do we live? The master is going away, yes, yes, we know about that, have known about it for nearly two thousand years now. But here is something we may not know: the master "puts his servants in charge, each with his [or her] own work."

The class that won't work except when Mrs. Jones is pacing up and down the aisles is a worthless class. The servant who can be trusted only when the master is present is a worthless servant. The faith that is vibrant only when the Savior stands beside us is worthless faith. The piety that knows no prayer other than "God, come and do something about your world" is worthless. Moral behavior that has no other basis than fear of the omnipresent gaze of God is worthless.

God's presence is decisive. The return of the master, whenever he returns, is a time for accounting, judgment. We are right to continue to sing about, pray for, and enjoy the presence of God when we get it here in bread and wine at this altar on Sunday or over coffee and cornflakes on Monday. Having experienced one advent of Christ, we are right to stand on tiptoes expecting the next.

But that doesn't change a thing in the meantime, which is the only time we have ever known. Whether the master is with us or not, present in Durham or absent in heaven, with us in Galilee or without us in Palm Beach, the master has put his servants in charge, each with his or her own work. Watch, therefore. You don't know when the master will come—in the evening, at midnight, in a few moments when you open your hands to receive blessed bread at the altar, or tomorrow morning at the office.

The kingdom of God, the presence of God in our world, is not only a matter of absence, painful, empty absence. It is also a matter of our being entrusted with work to do, responsibilities to be met, lives to be lived, children to be raised, exams to be taken, classes to be met, words to be spoken, prayers to be said, bread to be offered, deeds to be done. The master, the first time he was with us, put us, his servants, in charge, each with our own work, and told us to keep at it until he got back. We don't know when he will come and put us to the test, have us render account. "Of that day or that hour no one knows, not even the angels in heaven, nor the Son" (Mark 13:32).

All we know is that the kingdom of God is now. We need not wait until our prayers for presence are answered. And "Come, Thou Long-Expected Jesus" isn't an Advent wish, but a present fact. Already. Now. He has put his servants in charge, each with his or her own work. The kingdom of God is work entrusted to a bunch of servants. Now.

(Thanks to Bernard Brandon Scott, *Hear Then the Parable* [Minneapolis: Fortress Press, 1989], pp. 205–216, for his exegetical insights on this parable.)

Dear Will:

When I heard "Now" I was really quite taken with the sermon. However, for some reason I wanted to wait before responding until I had a chance to read it. It seemed to me the sermon was complex in terms of the kind of imagery it used and its interrelationship, and I really thought it was the kind I should read. I'm glad I waited, because on re-reading it several times I continue to be quite moved by the sermon, yet I'm beginning to realize why something about it was bothering me.

I take it that the basic strategy in the sermon is to help people identify with the eschatological tension that is involved in the Markan little apocalypse. I thought that it was probably a mistake for you not to situate the text within the apocalyptic claims of Mark 13. As it stands, you let the text be a parable abstracted from the quite dramatic imagery of the rest of Mark 13. I think that is important, because you need to show that the text functions within quite a different kind of subtext from the context you elicit at the beginning of the sermon.

For example, it is a very interesting strategy to help your hearers note that they identify with the servants in the text to begin with. Therefore, at the beginning you help us see that we identify with the little guys and the have-nots, and so are reading this text within the narratives of the American identification with the underdog. However, I'm not sure that should have been allowed to dominate the overriding theme of the sermon. The eschatological time that Jesus creates is of course quite a different time from the one most Americans assume as part of the underdog narrative.

That theme of the underdog you nicely subvert, however, by suggesting that the whole New Testament is concerned with the problem of absence. That was the theme that so struck me when I heard the sermon, and I wish you had done more with it. If you had, then you would have helped your hearers realize that the eschatological themes of the New Testament, and in particular their apocalyptic resonance, resituate our lives in terms of a different narrative from the one we normally embody, or perhaps better, that embodies us.

But you did not develop that theme with the power it deserves. You note that we've never known time with Jesus except the time of absence, and therefore there is a certain sense that as Christians we always live in Advent. Yet I don't think you emphasized enough the kind of absence we Christians live in. For example, one of the things you could have developed is how Jesus' presence creates an absence we have never known before. Just as we eat and drink with Jesus in the Eucharist, we also know that just to the extent that we find Jesus so present there, we also know how painful it is to find that presence absent in the rest of our lives.

It seems to me homiletically you could have developed the kind of experiences we all have where the powers of particular people have created absences that we would have never known without their particularity. For example, I often reflect on how much my friendship with an elderly friend means to me. As I watch him growing older

I realize that when he dies there will be an absence that cannot be made up. I would not live without his presence, and I will in a sense rejoice in the absence his death creates. For that absence is but the other side of the enjoyment of his presence. It creates a different time, and I shall always live in that time.

It is this kind of presence and absence that you needed to create in this sermon. It is not that Jesus has withdrawn through resurrection in a way that he is no longer present to us, but that the kind of presence that Jesus has created among us, the kind of presence that we constantly enjoy, creates an absence that we would not live without.

It's extremely important to develop that kind of dialectic for a sermon like this or you are going to reinforce the deistic presupposition that grips most of our lives. At best, most of us believe that God is a name of something that had to start it all, that might have been displayed in certain powerful lives but on the whole is absent. In the meantime we have to make up for that absence through our work. So the whole language of the test of servants that you use in the sermon can (and I know you were trying to avoid any such implications) underwrite moral bootstrapping. That is why the kind of absence that is produced is so important, because of the kind of presence that Jesus embodied.

Again we find you caught in the apologetic task of trying to elicit experiences that people have in common so that they will better be able to appreciate what eschatology is all about. But I think in the process you will underwrite senses of time that are contrary to those characteristic of the gospel. It is the time of the kingdom that is central here, not time in general. If the Gospels are primarily about Jesus' absence, it is because of the kind of presence the disciples discovered and we continue to discover.

While I do not want to say that the metaphor of test is

inappropriate for the eschatological tension, it doesn't seem appropriately developed in this sermon. The kind of test that confronts us is not one that contains problems for which there are right or wrong responses. Rather, it is like the kind of test that comes from being invited to be part of an adventure for which there are no right or wrong answers. So it is for a very particular kind of work that each of us is called, that is, part of the test of the kingdom. Again I think the eschatological focus must be kept at the forefront for a sermon like this to work.

For example, I note that you change the phrase "puts his servants in charge," to "puts his servants in charge, each with his *own* work." What is interesting is that the text doesn't say own. Indeed I think it is quite ambiguous in the text whose work it is that each servant takes up. I suspect that you were interpreting this text along the lines of the talents parable, but I'm not sure that is appropriate, as it is not the individual servant's work, but the *master's* work, that each of us is asked to take up. It doesn't mean that we are called to be good milkmaids and/or bankers, but rather that we are called to serve the kingdom well. It doesn't mean that our little task will bring in the kingdom, but that because the kingdom is present in the life, death, and resurrection of Jesus, all time has now been transformed so that we have tasks of the kingdom.

I liked very much how the sermon ends—in terms that the kingdom of God is now entrusted to a bunch of servants. I think that is exactly right, but then you should have displayed better what it meant to be servants in the kind of work we do. It is the work of the kingdom that comes through loving one another. Such love in a world of extraordinary violence and injustice can take the time to do those small things that God has made possible through the inauguration of this extraordinary kingdom.

In closing, I don't know whether I've criticized this sermon or not. It is a haunting sermon, and that denotes its power. It's the kind of sermon that reminds me that the kinds of examples we use are absolutely crucial. I realize that my substitution of your teacher example for my example of how presence creates absence is still a kind of experiential expressivist strategy, in Lindbeck's terms. In that sense it is not nonapologetic. But it certainly is a different kind of move to show how the kind of narrative embodied in the Gospel creates an experience that otherwise would not be possible. Of course I believe that is what the sermon is trying to do, and that is why I think it's so important that we attend to the examples.

Peace,

Stanley

CHAPTER 9

More

Third Sunday of Advent
Isaiah 61:1–4, 8–11

"The Spirit of the Lord God is upon me,
  because the Lord has anointed me
. . . to bring good news to the oppressed,
  to bind up the brokenhearted,
to proclaim liberty to the captives,
  and release to the prisoners;
to proclaim the year of the Lord's favor. . . .
They shall build up the ancient ruins,
  they shall raise up the former devastations. . . .
The Lord God will cause righteousness and praise
  to spring up before all the nations" (NRSV).

There is more to life than meets the eye. There is
more in our past than history can tell. There is more
going on in the present moment than we know. There is
more to our relationships with one another than we are
aware of. And the more we explore the mystery of ourselves, the more mysterious our selves become. Seldom
have we been content with what appeared on the sur-
face; we know there is more. Seldom have we felt fully
at ease in the present moment, sensing, however incho-
ately, that no matter how full our present, beyond the
now there is more. (See Wilfred Cantwell Smith, "Religion as Symbolism," *The Encyclopaedia Britannica,*
15th ed., vol. 1 [Chicago: Encyclopaedia Britannica Educational Corp., 1987], p. 299.)

We tend, if left to our own devices, toward reduction-
ism. Here in academia we ought to be exploring possibilities, enriching our sense of what is not known,

cultivating wonder. Alas, if left to our own devices, we reduce the cosmos to the periodic table. We explain human history by reducing it to the six causes of the Civil War, the main reason for the Great Depression, thirty true/false statements explaining the eighteenth century. In our better moments, when the modern analytic gives way to the eternal poetic, we know there is more.

When life is reduced to technique, six easy steps toward sure success, flattened to a series of problems to be solved, we become numbed, anesthetized against either real pain or true pleasure. The body adjusts, in the absence of expectation, to its cage. But occasionally someone manages to hit a nerve and we, twitching slightly in discomfort, suspect that there may be more.

The audience for this Advent text from Isaiah are the afflicted, the brokenhearted, the captives, those in prison, and mourners. In short, your average Durham December congregation. The people to whom these words are addressed are those who come to church out of a sometimes barely felt, sometimes fervently burning hope for more. The words also speak (though we know not how they will hear them) to those who have stopped coming to church because they have given up hoping for anything more.

Here is what Isaiah says: God has intervened, God has anointed One to take action. That action is political—release of prisoners, reparation for the ruined cities, justice. The intervention is announced by the poetical. It's just poetry here. Poetry with dangerous (dangerous for the establishment, that is) political repercussions. The "year of the Lord" which Isaiah announces is jubilee time, when everything to which the established political order would have us adjust is turned upside down, set right, and the devastated, empty streets of downtown Durham are transformed into a great festival.

When we were slaves in Egypt, God intervened, and we remember. We had learned to be content with our lot in Egypt. (At least in slavery our masters gave us three square meals a day.) But God intervened and led us out toward more. Intervention is needed again, some decisive intrusion that will enable new life and halt our march toward death. Israel and the church struggle to describe this intervention. Exodus. Bethlehem. Calvary. The upper room. The empty tomb. Without intervention, there is no hope, for there is no "more." And, thank God, because there is God, in circumstances of the worst brokenheartedness, captivity, imprisonment, and mourning, there is always more.

Isaiah speaks of a world beyond present arrangements, a world where there is good news, liberty, comfort, garlands, instead of ashes. This is biblical apocalyptic, Bible talk about the more beyond the now. It is daring, poetic, political speech, speech pushed to the boundaries in description of what God is breaking open among us, breaking open in dusty little out-of-the-way places like Bethlehem or Soweto. Isaiah's words refuse to abide within the confines of the rationality of the dominant society, refuse to be limited by common sense, NAS's "Canon of Western Literature." Apocalyptic speech breaks open.

It was Isaiah who taught Mary to sing apocalyptically, "My soul magnifies the Lord,/ . . . my spirit rejoices in God my Savior, .../he has scattered the proud, .../ he has put down the mighty from their thrones,/and exalted those of low degree;/he has filled the hungry with good things,/and the rich he has sent empty away" (Luke 1:46b–53).

When we come to church and are exposed to such speech from Isaiah or Mary, we are beckoned out beyond the world of predictability into another world of risk and gift, in which divine intervention enables new life to break our prosaic reductions, to subvert tamed expectations, to evoke fresh faith. Dangerous hope leads to daring resistance. Docility is no longer possible for those who heard tell of more.

Being interviewed on television, a group of Soviet Christian dissidents was asked by a reporter, "Well, what do you want? Why aren't Soviet Christians satisfied with the new freedoms that Gorbachev has given? Why won't you now soften your criticism and support the government?"

A Christian dissident responded, the translator explained, "He says they are not satisfied. He says they want more."

Anything less is trap and delusion. Sunday, at its best, is a summons toward more. But not just any old more. Our vague, frequently reoccurring, gnawing sense of need, which we so often attempt to assuage by more mere buying, accumulating, getting, and giving—particularly at this time of year—is articulated and reformed by the prophet as a groping after God and God's will. The "more" we desire is given a name, named "the year of the Lord's favor." The year in which God gets what God wants, when earth more closely resembles that which God first had in mind when God began forming nothing into something, less into more.

Poetic, apocalyptic, prophetic speech as that of Isaiah, or Mary, or an Advent hymn, doesn't just describe the world, it re-creates, makes a world. It is a world made open, with old, comfortable certitudes broken by the advent of a God who makes all things new. In the world where God comes, we are allowed to roam. Here is poetic imagination assaulting ideology. New configurations of life yet unformed, unthought, undreamed, now available.

"The Spirit of the Lord God is upon me, . . . good tidings to the afflicted; . . . the opening of the prison to those who are bound; . . . to give them a garland instead of ashes. . . . "

Here is Isaiah's poetic protest against religion reduced to slogan, morals, five fundamentals, bumper-sticker proverbs, thoughts for the day, religion relegated to the conventional, the boring rehash of the obvious and the already known. Here is protest against Sunday as adjustment to what is seen rather than probing of the more. We came to church for certitude, to touch base with the known, but apocalyptic speech goes beyond certitude. In the poetic, apocalyptic, Spirit-anointed space, possibility overwhelms necessity and we can breathe.

So we go forth after church. There are the same quarrels in the car on the way home, the same tensions over the dinner table, the same blue Monday. Now, however, we are aware of a new world, new hope, new possibility, new dreams, new hunger for something else—in short, we are aware of more. We see how greatly reduced, how tamed has been our truth. We, who have tasted new wine, now thirst for more.

The Prince of Darkness whispers, "adjust, adapt." The Prince wants to keep the world closed, for a closed world is easier to administer, and people without a future are more manageable than those with imagination.

Some Sundays when we gather, the Prince rules the roost. No new thing is uttered or heard. The pulpit is the place of platitudes, comfortable clichés, proverbs, slogans, and nothing more.

But sometimes, on a cold Sunday in December, we peek over the horizon, stand on tiptoes with Isaiah, and there is more. Somebody goes home from church newly discontent with present arrangements, hungry. Someone gets ready for more than just another Christmas. Advent becomes adventure. And we dare to wish for ourselves more, more for our world, more for others, and Isaiah laughs and Mary sings. Poetry has carried the day against prose, and the Prince knows that he has lost a little of his territory to its true Lord. The Lord's newly reclaimed territory is you.

"The kingdom of the world has become the kingdom of our Lord and of his Christ, and he shall reign for ever and ever" (Rev. 11:15).

Did you read in the paper about the man in a depressed region of Appalachia, a coal miner out of work for months, who caught his children on the back porch thumbing through a Sears catalog, wishing. He flew into a rage, switched their legs, tore the catalog to bits, and sat down in his yard and wept. He loved them so much, he couldn't bear to see them wish for more.

Did you read in the Bible about the young woman in a depressed region of Judea, a poor unmarried mother-to-be who was caught singing for more? "My soul magnifies the Lord, . . . for he who is mighty has done great things . . . . He has scattered the proud . . . , he has put down the mighty . . . , and exalted those of low degree; he has filled the hungry with good things."

Dear Will:

By God, I think you really pulled it off with "More." You really made the eschatological/apocalyptic language work without existentializing it. Admittedly, the beginning of the sermon seemed like a kind of existentializing when you pointed to our experience of always thinking that there is more to our past, to our loves, to ourselves.

But I think the way you pulled that back into the general text of the sermon transformed that sense of longing. What you did was not existentialize the eschatological so much as you showed its clear political implications. For example, the way that you reminded us in the university how we try to provide reductionistic accounts of the "more." You were right. Moreover, such reductionistic accounts are at the very heart of the contemporary university, insofar as we want to be a community of prose, not poetry. As a community of prose, of course, we serve the establishment you were so wonderfully critiquing.

It reminded me of MacIntyre's point in *After Virtue* that the fact-value distinction wasn't the result of epistemological developments, and then we got social orders commensurate with such a distinction. Rather the fact-value distinction was produced in order to legitimate the new power elite associated with managers and their priests, whom we call experts, who want to control the world without hope. Therefore I thought you were quite right to remind us how apocalyptic talk forces us into the world of risk, and in particular to associate that with the National Association of Scholars' attempt to limit the so-called canon.

I found particularly powerful, by the way, that phrase you used in the sermon that the body adjusts to whatever cage it is given. That was exactly the kind of poetry that you suggest apocalyptic gives us to rightly diagnose our condition. Also the cage image for me elicited that startling passage at the end of Max Weber's *Capitalism and the Spirit of Protestantism,* where he talks about how capitalism inextricably creates an iron cage from which there is no exit, since the very means to try to escape it only creates more cages.

Therefore you set it up wonderfully to show why there is no way out of such cages without intervention. Moreover, such intervention must come from a beyond that we Christians call God. So you elicited our sense of transcendence in a political context that nicely correlated with why poetry is the only way that such transcendence can be given expression.

One of the things I admire about this sermon, and many of your sermons, is how you have done your exegetical work without trying to call attention to it in the sermon itself. I think you were exactly right to associate the Isaiah text with jubilee. You mention the notion of jubilee, but you don't try to explain it. It simply stands there as a reminder that Israel was never limited by past forms of injustice, since they were under the legislation of the jubilee to overturn their social order in terms of past injustices at least every fifty years. Of course it can always be objected they didn't do that, but the fact that they had it makes all the difference.

The political context of the whole sermon was carried out wonderfully when you reminded us at the end that this newly acquired territory that God creates through intervention is called "you." We are now those who are God's weapons against the Prince of Darkness. Your appeal to Sunday as the time God has created to make us a people who always want more, even after we get out of prison, seems to me just right. The appeal to Sunday seemed to be particularly powerful as you note that our apocalyptic language isn't about describing the world, even our most existentially compelling experiences, but re-creates a world. Surely that is what Sunday is about, as through the creation of that day we Christians know we live in a whole new time. Sunday is risk.

Finally the thing I liked about this sermon is how you blended the Isaiah text with Mary's Magnificat. Finding a way to help people hear the Magnificat as a war song of our God is hard once we have so sentimentalized it. You did it in an extraordinary way, particularly with the coal miners' story about his children reading the Sears catalog. If I had used that story, I would have been tempted to explain it, but thank God you didn't. For example, you didn't say that our God loves us so much that God is willing even to have us die, to be hurt, rather than to be captured by the hopes of this world. So Mary's Song stands as the triumph of God against the deadening of imagination in this world by those who think we have no future other than the violence "necessary to get things done." Mary is our alternative, just as Israel is our alternative. God turns out to be a God of risk and, believe it or not, we are just that risk. What an extraordinary thing for God to do!

I have been thinking about Eudora Welty's comment to a reporter about where she got her ideas for her extraordinary short stories. She said, "Why, I just read *The Oxford Times*." She picked up a copy to show the reporter and said, "See! Right here on the front page it says, 'Man Kills Wife After Coming Home from Sunday School.' Who could have ever thought that up?" That is how we need to think about the imagination and how God forms it. What is extraordinary is that we keep thinking we have to imagine how we would create the world if we only had power. What God has already done has given us such compelling "facts" as exodus, exile, crucifixion, resurrection, and church, and we still can't believe that those are our imagination. That is why we don't need to existentialize the gospel; all we need to do is let it confront us as you did in this wonderful sermon.

You have a hopeful sermon, and you never even suggested explicitly it was about hope.

Peace,

Stanley

CHAPTER 10

Here

Fourth Sunday in Advent
Luke 2:1–20

*"Joseph also went from the town of Nazareth
in Galilee to Judea, to the city of David called
Bethlehem, because he was descended from
the house and family of David. He went to
be registered with Mary, to whom he was engaged
and who was expecting a child"* (NRSV).

The Seekers Sunday School Class was discussing what to do about Christmas. Gladys suggested that the class restore the custom of adopting a needy family, buying them clothes, food, what they needed, and taking the stuff by on Christmas Eve.

Good idea, Gladys. Adopt a needy family for Christmas. *The Durham Morning Herald* has a list of them.

"Not so fast, Gladys," said Martha. "Christmas food baskets for the poor went out with the hoola hoop. Food-basket charity is degrading, ineffective—the good old Seekers Class assuaging its guilt with a once-a-year trip across the tracks to do a little something for one poor family."

"Well, what do you suggest that we do for the poor?" snapped Gladys.

"We need to address the systemic causes of poverty and work for structural change that helps a whole society rather than preparing a food basket for one poor family. Get to the root causes, the systemic sources. No wonder the church is ignored. It's always loving a neighbor and forgetting about the neighborhood."

How do you think the Seekers Class should spread its Christmas charity? Most of us educated, enlightened types agree with Martha. In the last couple of decades, charity has become a dirty word. Rather than one-to-one, face-to-face food baskets for the poor, most of us now believe that we ought to spread our Christian concern to as many people as possible by changing the structures that produce poverty—show the right attitude about poverty by rights fights rather than Christmas food baskets, right giving.

When one of our students asked a professor to give a Saturday to work on Duke's Habitat for Humanity house, the professor replied:

"I don't work for Habitat for Humanity because I don't believe it solves the problem of homelessness to build just one house at a time. If you really care about homelessness, you ought to work for a new senator in Washington."

See? With Martha we have been taught to look past the sad lot of the Joneses toward more universal, society-wide concern for the less fortunate. Greatest good for the greatest number and all that.

Big. General. Universal.

And yet, the Christmas story is anything but big, general, or universal. The nativity story, which we just read from Luke, is decidedly small, specific, and particular. It's not about the whole human race, it's about people, real people, with real names like Quirinius, Joseph, Mary. It doesn't begin with, "Once upon a time, in a land far away, there was a king." That's the way fairy tales begin, not Bible stories. Bible stories begin with,

"In those days a decree went out from Caesar Augustus.
. . . This was the first enrollment, when Quirinius was
governor of Syria. And all went to be enrolled. . . .
Joseph went up from Galilee, from the city of Nazareth,
to Judea, to the city of David, which is called Bethlehem."

See? Specific. Particular. Not a "once upon a time,"
timeless, eternal. You can date it. Quirinius was governor of Syria. You can take a road map and follow Mary
and Joseph's journey. Galilee, to Nazareth, to Bethlehem.

A fairy tale happens to anybody, anyplace or anytime.
But not Bible stories.

And this particularity, this smallness and specificity,
is not just a characteristic of biblical narratives like the
nativity story. It's built into the Christian faith itself. I
have this friend, a professor, who has become active in
his church again after a long absence. I asked him how
his newfound commitment to the church was going. "I
agree with the general principles of the church, the
church's goals, programs, you know. But I don't like
those stories."

"Stories?" I asked.

"Yeah, those Bible stories. They make it all sound so
limiting, so concrete."

And I suppose, if we were as honest as my friend,
we've all felt that way about the Christian faith. It's
these stories, like the one about Mary and Joseph on
their way to Bethlehem during the Quirinius administration.

What we prefer on Christmas is John's high-sounding
rhetoric of the incarnation. "The Word became flesh
and dwelt among us, full of grace and truth; we have
beheld his glory" (John 1:14). See? None of those
messy details about Quirinius's enrollment. No Mary.

125

No Joseph. No detours through dusty, conflict-ridden, backwater Bethlehem on our way up to the rarefied reaches of yuletide sentiment.

We love to drink in religion as clear liquor, from which the gross particularities of history and geography have been distilled. We thrill to the enunciation of universal, timeless truth, relevant to humanity in every age. And yet here we are, on the eve of Christmas, ready to receive homiletic urging toward universal human love, and all we get is a hasty trip from nowhere Nazareth to backwater Bethlehem, made by a Jewish couple named Mary and Joseph during the reign of Augustus.

Like my friend, we affirm the general principles of the faith, are in broad agreement with the church's goals, but our problem is with these stories, so concrete, particular.

Like Martha, we are concerned about others in the broadest, most general sort of way, concerned when standing in the voting booth rather than standing on their front door stoop bearing a basket of canned goods and a turkey for Christmas.

And yet—if we are to love as God loves, judging from Luke's account of the nativity, then somehow we must learn to love with a particularity and specificity that make us squirm.

The Bible does not say, "God is love"—abstract affirmation floating above human time and place. It says that God loves Israel, God chose Mary, God spoke to Joseph, God loved Jesus, God called the church as scandalously particular. Rarely does the Bible speak in timeless generality. More typically, the Bible speaks in the way of today's text, God going to specific people, at particular times, in particular places. The implication: *particular times, specific people living in particular places like Bethlehem matter to God.*

There is an unrelenting, passionate particularity in the way God intrudes into human life. Abstract, general (even if high-sounding) ideas rarely have the power to grasp or to invigorate us. It is only in the particular and the specific that lives are engaged. Here.

"I am sending flowers to a person who is a representative, in a general sort of way, of the highest and best human aspirations."

No. When we're in love, one of the reasons why our love so transforms us, engages every waking moment, is that we love this person, the way she walks, her favorite food, the sound of her name. Jane. J-a-n-e. She need not stop being Jane and blend into the great, gray lump called "the human race." If she did, she wouldn't be half so lovable.

God's love invades our time and place, with similarity, specificity, particularity, and partiality. It wasn't that the "Word became flesh" once upon a time, someplace, to some people. It was that Jewish Mary of Nazareth, Galilee, had a baby named Jesus in Bethlehem. Here.

To witness such passionate divine intensity about the specific and the particular is to realize the possibility that this may just be the way God always loves us and intends for us so to love others. Because God does not disdain being born in a place like Bethlehem, to people like Mary and Joseph, there is a better than even chance that God might condescend to get mixed up among people like you and me in a place like Durham. Here.

That's what makes God's love so discomforting. Its particularity. John's "The Word became flesh" is more comfortable than Luke's Bethlehem, Nazareth, Mary, and Joseph. Luke's story discomforts because it challenges our assumption that our daily lives really don't matter. We resist loving and being loved as God loves because there is something reassuring in the thought that our little lives don't matter that much to God, certainly not enough to disrupt us during tax season by an unexpected pregnancy or a voice from heaven while we are doing our bit with the sheep on the night shift. Here.

Oh, we love to come to church and be served a soufflé of universal principles, general thoughts, abstract-ideas puff pastry. Luke says that's not God's way with us. Instead of lofty, fluffy platitudes about the human race we are confronted with a poor Jewish carpenter and his young, pregnant-out-of-wedlock wife, looking for a place to spend the night in Bethlehem. Rather than sociological abstractions about the systemic causes of injustice, we are made to look at the Joneses, the way their eyes turn down as we hand over the food basket filled with canned goods we didn't need, their gratitude exceeded by their resentment. It is one thing to love humanity. It's another thing to love the Joneses, to have our hypocritical platitudes deflated by their justified resentment. Here.

Hate appears to be similarly disrupted by the particular and the specific. What do you think when you hear the word Iraq? Lawless aggressors? Terrorists led by a crazed fanatic no better than Hitler?

But picture in your mind an eighteen-year-old from Baghdad, shivering in the desert, in green fatigues, a long way from home, snapshot of his girlfriend in one pocket, photo of his mother in another, staring across desert wastes at another eighteen-year-old from Birmingham, pictures of his girlfriend in one pocket, of his mother in another.

When facing only the universal, it's easier to pull the trigger, isn't it? Perhaps that's why our leaders speak in generalities of violation of international law, the rules of a new world order, rather than particularities, specificities. President Johnson damaged public support for another war, not in a desert, but in a jungle, when L.B.J. said in specific candor, "War is sending one mother's son to kill some other mother's son."

Of course, if that mother's son from Baghdad is a Muslim, he doesn't know Luke 2, doesn't know it's Christmas. But we know that story, and it says that God loves him as much as God loves us, with scandalous particularity, face-to-face, one at a time. Here.

It is only as we learn to love others, in the same manner as God has loved us, face-to-face, one at a time, with risky specificity and particularity, that God's way has a chance in a violent, nameless, faceless world, a world made all the more violent because of its facelessness, its namelessness, its placelessness.

When God came among us, in the flesh, Emmanuel, God didn't hover over the whole world. God came to Bethlehem. God did not appear as an idea or a program. God came to Mary and Joseph. When God decided to challenge the military might of Ceasar's legions, God did not come as some new social strategy. God came as a baby named Jesus.

That's this God's way of doing things, the first Christmas or this Christmas. So you'd better pay attention to your life, particularly its ordinariness, its specificity—better notice the names, look into the faces, for this is how God comes among us, one by one. Here.

The ordinary, specific, little things you do, like having babies, going on holiday trips to visit relatives over in Bethlehem, paying taxes, are redeemed. This is where you can expect to be grasped by God. Here.

I was at a conference of learned theologians where a speaker categorized the gospel as "radical obedience to

God's program of justice, righteousness, and peace for the whole world."

One of my colleagues responded that in a little town in Ohio, early morning, a woman is getting out of bed, looking forward to another day of caring of her retarded adult daughter before she goes to work at the local diner. For this woman, the greatest act of "radical obedience" to Jesus Christ is when she says a little prayer, just before she gets out of bed, asking a loving God to help her make it one more day.

Emmanuel. God with us. Here.

Dear Will:

The best thing about "Here" is how you linked politics and theology. By beginning with the Seekers Class example, you nicely showed how our political attitudes mirror our theological presuppositions, and vice versa. Your sermon reminded me of the wonderful article by Christina Sommers, who argues that holding the right political opinions has become the new form of self-righteousness. It doesn't matter whether you yourself are charitable as long as you have the correct political attitudes and are willing to exercise them by being on the left wing of the Democratic Party. I thought you critiqued that about as well as it can be critiqued.

I do think you need to be careful, however, about the general juxtaposition of particularity to universality. To think you must choose between the particular and the universal is the way the Enlightenment wants you to think. The difficulty with that is it makes it sound as if you are giving up on something called universality in favor of something called particularity, when in fact you are saying that those are both false abstractions. The way I often put it is, what could be more universal than Jesus? I remember in a conversation recently you pointed out that those who keep talking about "public theology" want to talk about justice, because they think justice is more accessible to anyone. Yet they often discover that nothing is more controversial and unable to elicit agreement than an abstraction like justice. As long as we are going to be in controversy, we might as well talk about Jesus.

I thought that you nicely juxtaposed the notion of myth to story in that regard. However, just as we have to be careful with juxtaposition of particularity and universality, so we have to be on our guard about that distinction between myth and story. I thought the way you did it was about as well as it can be done, but you want to be careful not to make the gospel hinge on a genre distinction between story and myth. The fundamental difference between the gospel and myths is we believe that Mary was carrying the Messiah and not Athena.

Notice, for example, that after you pointed out so nicely that the Bible does not speak of God as love, but rather that God loves Mary or Joseph or Jesus, you then suggest the rhetorical question: And what is the implication of this? That question can be deeply misleading, because it makes it sound as if the story about Mary has an implication beyond the story about Mary. You said the implication is that God always loves us particularly. That sounds like a point beyond the story, when I know that is exactly what you don't want to invite. Our problem in all this is that we keep being caught by the very language we are trying to fight. I do it all the time in my own work, and I don't think there is any easy solution.

By the way, I loved the language that God invades us with particularity of people like Mary and/or Jane. The language of invasion denotes exactly the kind of violent engagement that it seems we must talk about if we are

131

rightly to understand how God has the power to call us beyond our limits.

I was a bit worried about your juxtaposition of the Gospel of John with the Gospel of Luke. While no doubt you are right in terms of the general images of those two Gospels, it is nonetheless the case that John is just as particular in the first two chapters as the Gospel of Luke. It is just the way we read *logos* that makes us think that John is any less particular than Luke.

I thought in that regard you might have talked about concreteness rather than particularity and/or universality. In particular it occurred to me that what was missing is the practice of Eucharist as part of the Duke Chapel service. There is all the concreteness of the *logos* one needs. If you had been able to say that it is from this that we know we worship no universal God, but a God who is present right here and now, we then would be able rightly to understand that the God we face is the God who has made himself present in this Jewish carpenter.

Again I am so aware of how sermons are inextricably context-dependent. It occurred to me that one of the things you could have done is use what you were saying to challenge those of us who love to worship at Duke Chapel. One of the reasons we love Duke Chapel is that on the whole we don't know many of the people around us. Of course that is not quite true, as we often recognize one another as part of the so-called Duke community. However, we like Duke Chapel because we can come and worship there with no one having much of a hold on us. So Duke Chapel represents the universal ideal that we can come together as strangers and still be bound together in the worship of God.

There is something right about that insofar as we know that God makes us more of a community than we would have ever been through Eucharist, but it can also be very self-deceptive. As we worship in Duke Chapel we lose exactly the concreteness of the person next to us so necessary for worship.

Of course it is that kind of concreteness that also bothers us so much, since as we know people more it is as likely that we will hate them as that we will love them. I loved the illustration about war and how war, particularly in modernity, is all the more possible exactly because we fight for abstractions. War that is fought for territory or for the destruction of the enemy is so much healthier than war that is fought for something called democracy, when no one has any idea of what it might be. It seemed to me that someone could challenge your view that the Iraqi soldier and the American soldier are able to kill each other exactly because they are in the grip of universal abstractions. People are also able to kill one another because they know one another so concretely. That is why the violence that is often the most severe and destructive occurs in families. If wars were fought with the kind of intensity of familial violence, I suspect few of us would be around today. That doesn't undercut your primary point that just is a way of remembering that nothing can be more violent than our particular loves.

However, I thought the way that you brought that around to suggest that it was Jesus who was God's answer to Caesar was about as powerful a way to make the overall claims of the sermon as I know. Moreover, the close connection of that claim with the woman who cares for her mentally handicapped daughter day in and day out seems to me to be just right. It is that care that is God's peace, as we then have an alternative to war.

I think the strength of this sermon can be illuminated by the very fact that after it I liked singing "O Little Town of Bethlehem." I hate "O Little Town of Bethlehem." It is one of the most clichéd hymns we have, and I think of it as inextricably sentimental. However, it suddenly had new vigor for me by the time you had finished this sermon. I was so pleased to think that even though this Bethlehem looked a lot like a German town, it was good that Jesus got himself born there. Your concreteness worked, and I rejoiced in it.

Again you succeeded in narrating our lives into Jesus' life by reminding us that our forms of concreteness only make sense as seen through God's story. It is a hard task to accomplish that, but I think you did it wonderfully well in this Advent/Christmas sermon. I think a lot about your claim that I don't appreciate the art of sermons, and on the whole I think you are right. But I thought this sermon was wonderfully artful as you juxtaposed stories and images throughout that carried the gospel with power and illuminating simplicity.

Peace,

Stanley

Postscript

William H. Willimon

Some time ago I overheard two musicians at our Chapel discussing the possible performance of a particular piece of contemporary music. "Could we muster the orchestra and singers to tackle that piece?" asked one of the other.

"Oh, sure. No problem getting the musicians," said the other. "The problem would be in finding the necessary audience. I don't think we have yet developed the tastes of the people of Durham to the point where we could ask the musicians to go through all that work and expect their efforts to be heard." It had not occurred to me how dependent musicians are on people who are trained to hear their music.

Take that conversation as a synopsis of what Stanley's thoughts have evoked in me concerning the evangelistic challenge of preaching to strangers.

I have long suspected that many congregations get the preachers they deserve. Faithful preaching is frighteningly dependent on faithful listening. In my last congregation I had a woman, a schoolteacher, who made it her business, when she felt I had struggled well with a sermon, to comment after the sermon. It was her way of encouraging me. It was also her way of doing what she could to protect herself from bad sermons. Good preaching requires good listening.

When Stanley Hauerwas is doing the listening, well, that's some conversation! Because Stanley is a friend, his responses tend to be considerably more pointed than the conventional, "Nice sermon, preacher," a comment that more often than not ends the conversation rather than aids it. Because Stanley is a theologian, he is called by God and the church to tell us what we are actually saying, and neglecting to say, when we preach and listen to sermons. I was willing to do this book with Stanley, to expose my theological nakedness to his penetrating gaze, because, for my money, few theologians are better able than Stanley to point their finger directly to what ails us.

In his Introduction to this book, Stanley says that, in beginning to read through my sermons, "something was missing." There is much that is missing in Stanley's analysis of what may be happening when I preach. He does not know, cannot know, the particular pastoral ecology in which I work, the five-minute conversation with a freshman that helped determine the direction of "Ordinary People," the hospital visit with a dying old man that became the catalyst for "More." When Stanley focuses on a sermon he acts as if he is doing a book review, cutting the sermon out of its liturgical context. To me, many of his criticisms of "The Day of the Lord" were addressed by the stunning contemporary anthem which the choir sang (with drums) immediately before the sermon. And it makes a great deal of difference (at least to me), that my "Freedom" was immediately followed by the congregation's singing of "Make Me a Captive, Lord." Oh, well, a sermon critic can't do everything, and nobody ever accused Stanley of aesthetic sensitivity. He found that one thing that was missing when he read my sermons was the "inextricably dramatic character of the sermon," the "live word," that which Gerhard Ebeling would have described as the "word-event" when the word is actually *heard.* Yet Ebeling's description would not suit Stanley because of its incipient existentializing of preaching. Ebeling's "event" is too momentary, individualized, subjectivized, just the sort of theology that, in Stanley's opinion, is created by those who no longer have the church.

In his Introduction, Stanley cites George Lindbeck and Alasdair MacIntyre as helpful in recognizing the dependence of Christian speaking on a community that knows how and for what purpose it is to listen. I am also reminded of the work of Duke's literary critic, Stanley Fish, who speaks of the text's need for "interpretive communities" in order for a text to have meaning. Fish observes that it makes a great deal of difference, in reading a given text, what my interpretive community has enculturated me to expect of that text. "Skilled reading," says Fish, "is usually thought to be a matter of discerning what is there, . . . [but] it is a matter of knowing how to *produce* what can thereafter be said to be there. Interpretation is not the art of construing but the art of constructing. Interpreters do not decode poems; they make them."[1]

Upon first reading Fish, I wanted to challenge him. As a preacher I am often struck, as I look at a given text for preaching, by the sheer "otherness" of a text, the way it comes upon me, challenges me, assaults me with its claims. Some of the best sermons in this collection reveal the preacher's shock and amazement upon being met by a text, an amazement that challenges Fish's contention that "what is there" in a text is not so important as the ways I as a preacher have been conditioned "how to *produce* what can thereafter be said to be there."

Yet, Stanley Hauerwas's commentary on my preaching certainly suggests that formation by an interpretive community makes all the difference in preaching. He cites Tillich as someone who preached not only to but more importantly *from* a community (the German university first, the American university second), which led him to approach a text from the conviction that it must be translated into modern thought (i.e., existentialism) to be understood, that the text's "practical implications" would need to be explained by a modern preacher, and that the only possible audience for a text were those already so well formed in their subjectivities that no text could challenge them.

My own encounter with a biblical text is dependent on that interpretive community that taught me to read the Bible as scripture. For me even to say that I am in an "encounter" with a text is testimony to what I have been enculturated to expect the Bible to do to me and to my fellow listeners. Plenty of Shakespeare's texts are as strange as those in the Bible. The difference is that we Christians are busy trying to live and to die by the Bible in a way that we are not with the plays of Shakespeare, so the "strangeness" is of a very different order.

So preaching is dependent on a listening community, and how well it has learned to hear scripture preached as scripture, as canon, as the rule for faith and practice, as that master story that subsumes and thereby transforms all other stories! As preacher I not only speak to that community but I am part of it, so it will make a great deal of difference under what sort of language game we have gathered on Sunday, by what rules we shall play. In Stanley's mind, I have often been guilty, in my Sunday preaching, of playing by the wrong set of rules, of speaking more out of one interpretive community (the modern American university) when I should have been exploring what it meant to have been baptized into a very different community (church), which listens to these ancient Near Eastern texts as *scripture*. To be in church on a Sunday morning is to be caught in a clash between differing interpretive communities. Because most of us have spent much of our lives being conditioned by interpretive communities other than the church, if a pastor's preaching does not at least occasionally sound odd, make us feel like strangers, then there is a good chance the pastor has got it wrong. Which brings us to what really appears to be missing in these sermons as Stanley has heard them and as I have preached them—*the church,* at least the church as it can be seen, which for Wesleyans like Stanley and me is the only church. Thus have we called this collection of sermons and responses *Preaching to Strangers.*

In his Introduction, Stanley described Duke Chapel as a unique place in which to preach. But is it really? I suspect that many preachers know what it means, Sunday after Sunday, to preach to those who are "just passing through," tourists who share no stories or tradition other than that they share neither story nor tradition. Here is where I hope the homiletical struggles portrayed in this book have hit a nerve with my fellow preachers. Barbarians our listeners may not be, but they are still strangers. Seen from this perspective, evangelistic preaching (I did not call Duke Chapel an "evangelical tent" but an *evangelistic* tent. I think there is a difference) is preaching that offers, in the name of Christ, *hospitality to the stranger.*

As Hauerwas notes, Christian conversation with strangers can be dangerous. I did not learn the danger of such preaching from Stanley but from Luke.[2] In Luke's Acts, he is obviously concerned with preaching to strangers— some of them fellow Jews, some Gentiles. Throughout Acts, Luke depicts Christians as people who will talk to anybody, even Gentiles, at any time or place. The trouble with speaking to Gentiles is that you can't quote scripture to them. If you do, you have to spend a great deal of time unpacking it; so not too many Gentiles get converted by the preachers in Acts and, when they are converted, Luke generally chalks it up as a completely unexpected work of the Spirit which dumbfounds the preacher as much as anybody.

In Luke's view, most of the really exciting things that happen in preaching, and nearly all the truly dangerous things, occur in missionary or evangelistic preaching. Out on the fringes, when one is struggling to speak about Jesus to those who have not heard (strangers), evangelism is always prone to degenerate into apologetics. So Luke's preachers expect and receive as much rejection from their listeners as acceptance and, time and again, they teach. They spend as much time teaching as preaching because they know that evangelism may be one of the most self-threatening activities of the church. It is so easy to get it all wrong. We end up evangelizing people into a linguistically accommodated church that Jesus never really wanted.

Most of our preaching called evangelistic is really apologetic. Tillich is us all over—on TV, certain popular banalities offered as gospel; in a university chapel, the subjectivities of bourgeois high culture delivered in a well-modulated voice. Hauerwas accuses me of existentializing eschatology, being experiential-expressivist when I ought to know better, and being far too gracious about God's grace. Of course, he is right. Open your door to strangers, you may be converted by them rather than convert them. You go out to love people only to be seduced by them.

Yet at least give me credit for knowing that the main issue is conversion. As Stanley notes, Christianity is a way of life that one cannot know except through conversion. I cannot know Christian discipleship by having Jesus translated into the language of psychological self-esteem any more than I can know French by reading *Madame Bovary* in an English translation. Most of us have been so well converted into modern, Western ways of knowing and living that we do not even know we have been converted, thus making it appear to us that Christianity is an odd perspective on life to which one must get acclimated, whereas our present cultural situation is normality that just is.

Who told Stanley that the people who congregate at Duke Chapel on Sunday are "strangers"? How do they know that they are strangers? Stanley complains that they are without story or tradition, but he does not know that story and tradition are essential for community (no, *true* stories are essential for truthful communities), except that he has been taught that by his life in the church.

Most of my Sunday congregation probably thinks that its lack of common story and tradition is the normal human condition. Our culture has found that people can be better managed and manipulated if they are told that their most important human characteristic is their detached subjectivity. Ironically, Western culture has succeeded in rendering us into a herd by convincing us that we are individuals who are obligated to no story, no tradition, no community other than the obligation to make up our own minds. Jesus is thus reduced to only another sometimes interesting opinion about which we are urged to make up our minds, to "make a decision for Christ" as the Evangelicals say.

How do I know that these people who sit in front of me are "strangers" unless the gospel teaches me what there is about me that makes *me* strange? I may think that they are strange because they have not been blessed, as Stanley, with a Texas accent and I, with a Southern accent. But no, they are strangers simply because Jesus Christ has also died for them, called them to be disciples, and they don't know it. Worst of all, *I* don't know it. That is to say, I persist in addressing them as if the main factor that potentially unites us is our "common humanity," which only awaits recognition through the sermon. So I begin sermons by pointing to our common enslavement, or universal depression, or lust, or whatever, then I name the gospel as a better way to deal with these common problems. Christianity is thus reduced to a mere matter of being awakened to what we already know. As his responses to many of my sermons show, Stanley has caught me in the act of apologetics time and again. *Mea culpa.* Alas, the one who requires gospel transformation is I, the preacher. I know that my congregation are "strangers" in those moments when I recognize my own strangeness, not so much my estrangement from the congregation (I am more their brother than I admit) but my estrangement from the gospel, from the life, death, and resurrection of the One who came to us as stranger, One so strange that we naturally had to kill him, only to have him return to us, forgive us, and call us to be his friends (an act that made him the ultimate stranger to us).

Having been received by him, despite all my enmity to his good news, is, so far as I know, the only basis by which I can receive others, recognizing these erstwhile strangers as brothers and sisters in Christ, enjoying again that cosmic normality which he meant for us to have when he created us and called us his handiwork, that cosmic normality (or at least its foretaste) which is called *church.*

So we return to the main thing missing in these sermons. There is not much wrong with these sermons, despite Stanley's criticisms, that can't be cured by a good dose of the church. *Christian* preaching requires transformation, initiation, in short, baptism, if it is to be heard. My sermons at their best are a testimony *of* the baptized to how wonderfully strange, surprising, and adventuresome is life after baptism and *to* the unbaptized about a way of life in Christ that is more a political matter of "Will you join up?" than a merely intellectual debate over "Do you agree?" To those who are baptized, sermons at their best are an invitation to continue to explore the practical significance of our baptism (as Luther said, baptism takes only a few minutes to do but your whole life to finish). To those who have not been baptized, sermons ought at least to point to the embodiment of Christian discipleship in the lives of ordinary Christians past and present, in the hope that what the unbaptized see and hear will not be so boring as to be, by its boringness, an insult to Jesus.

When Stanley and I wrote *Resident Aliens,*[3] I was sometimes asked by fellow pastors who read the book, "Why are you so enamored of the church? Duke Chapel is a long way from the typical parish church." Indeed, it is. Perhaps my vantage point of a pulpit a long way from the church gives me the opportunity to see how important a continuing, struggling, witnessing, converting community is for the proclamation of the gospel, to see again how dependent are we preachers on a group of people whose daily struggle to embody the gospel makes credible our efforts to speak the gospel. Fellow preachers might be surprised how tough it is to preach in Duke Chapel—even with the 210-foot steeple, 150-member choir, and four big organs.

My sermons at their worst are the occasionally alluring thoughts of a person who tells us, albeit in often artful ways, that which we already know even without knowing the church. In wanting so much to lean over "to speak to the world," I sometimes fall in.

In moments when I recognize my own infidelity, I know that such recognition has come only as grace, a gift. In the case of these sermons, that grace has a name and a face called Stanley. His friendship becomes for me, the preacher, a weekly reminder of how frighteningly dependent I am, as a preacher, on the church to listen, to embody in life, far better than I, the truth of which I so often only speak, the truth whose face and name is Jesus, the

Christ. Stanley's responses remind me that, as preacher and as listener, friends in Christ, what we are about is a mutual struggle to be faithful, a struggle so odd from the viewpoint of the world, it is prone to failure and therefore an occasion for forgiveness. I can forgive Stanley for making a living by criticizing preachers (grace is so amazing!) if he can forgive me for getting the gospel wrong when he, trying to be a faithful Christian *and* a university professor, so desperately deserves to hear the gospel on Sunday. Take our friendship, and this dialogue, as a microcosm, a little church within the church, of what it feels like to speak and to listen as Christians today, to have once been strangers who are now, by God's grace, church.

William H. Willimon

NOTES

1. Stanley Fish, *Is There a Text in This Class?* (Cambridge, Mass.: Harvard University Press, 1980), pp. 326–327.
2. William H. Willimon, *Acts: A Commentary for Interpretation* (Louisville, Ky.: Westminster/John Knox Press, 1989).
3. Stanley Hauerwas and William H. Willimon, *Resident Aliens: Life in the Christian Colony* (Nashville: Abingdon Press, 1990).